RADICAL
WALKING
TOURS OF
NEW
YORK
CITY

RADICAL WALKING TOURS OF NEW YORK CITY

BRUCE KAYTON

MAPS BY RENÉE MICHAELS

SEVEN STORIES PRESS / NEW YORK

A Seven Stories Press First Edition

In the U.K.:
Turnaround Publisher Services Ltd., Unit 3, Olympia Trading
Estate, Coburg Road, Wood Green, London N22 6TZ, U.K.

In Canada:
Hushion House, 36 Northline Road, Toronto, Ontario M4B 3E2,
Canada

Library of Congress Cataloging-in-Publication Data

Kayton, Bruce
    Radical walking tours of New York City / Bruce Kayton. — A
Seven Stories press 1st ed.
    p.   cm.
    ISBN 1-888363-66-5 (paper)
    1. New York (N.Y.)—Tours. 2. Walking—New York (State)—
New York—Guidebooks. 3. Social movements—New York (State)—
New York—History. 4. Radicalism—New York (State)—New York—
History. I. Title
F128.18.K38 1998
917.47'10443—dc21   97-50424
                                                        CIP

Seven Stories Press
140 Watts Street
New York, NY 10013
http://www.sevenstoriescom/

Printed in the U.S.A.

10 9 8 7 6 5 4 3 2 1

*Dedicated to all of those
who were born in the wrong era*

CONTENTS

ACKNOWLEDGMENTS

Many people have contributed both to the book and the success of *Radical Walking Tours* in an era when the "experts" claim there's no interest in left-wing politics. I would like to thank my "regulars," who have come on each of my tours and/or helped get the tours off the ground in the early years: Mark Rembe, Adam Cooper, Pat Colucci, Frank Richards, Francine Marchese, Phebe B., Todd Eaton, Mordechai Moore, Mary Lou Manning, Barry and Lindsay, Bob C., and Adam and Rose.

I thank all my fellow tour guides and historians who generously helped me over the years, in this most solitary of professions, and made me feel like a *real* tour guide: The monthly crowd that meets at the Cedar Tavern on University Place ("The Algonquin Club of the 90s"—Marvin Gelfand, Peter Selwyn, Val Ginter, Joyce Mendolsohn, Harriet Kram-Davis, James Kaplan, Margie Berk and Joe Zito), Ed O'Donnell of Big Onion Tours for advice and tips; Radical Walking Tour Guides Bob Erler, Scott Lewis, Bob Palmer, and Gene Glickman, in whose footsteps I figuratively and sometimes literally followed; and Dr. Sherrill D. Wilson for always helping me with African-American history, and the African Burial Ground. The tours might not have gotten off the ground without the support of WBAI (99.5 FM), the best radio station in the country, and more specifically without the initial support of Amy Goodman, Bernard White, Anthony Sloane (he's from the Bronx!), and Scott Somers (of *Housing Notebook*) over the years.

In no particular order, like my walking tours, the following individuals and groups have either helped me get started

9

or inspired me along the way: Pat D., the Democratic
Socialists of America and the Socialist Labor Party for that
early radical education, author William Lorenz Katz, the
Committee In Solidarity with the People of El Salvador (for
whom I gave my first free tours in 1990 at the invitation of
Marcia Lifschitz—some 200 tours ago), Marshall Dubin, ACT-
UP, WHAM!, Paul Poulos and Rochelle Semel, the Industrial
Workers of the World, countless librarians all over the city
(especially at the Forty-second Street Library in Manhattan,
the Tamiment Institute, the Schomburg Center for Research
in Black Culture and the Seward Park Library), Bob Fass, Bill
Weinberg, Peter Lamborn Wilson, Coca Crystal, Anne Rosen-
Noran, Tuli Kupferberg, Chris Flash and "The Shadow,"
Esther Kaplan and Jews for Racial and Economic Justice,
Richard Wandel of the National Museum of Lesbian and Gay
History, David McReynolds, Steve Ben-Israel, Jenya Cassidy,
Cecelia Cortez for starting it all, The New School For Social
Research and Associate Dean for Academic Affairs Sandra
Fargani, the Jewish Radical Education Project (specifically
Robert Wolfe and Miriam Steinberg), Yusef Jones, Harriet
Tanzman, the Marxist School, Lee Brozgold, my brother
David for Radical Walking Tours's Web site, Moses (the very
first Jewish walking tour guide), The New York Labor History
Association, Safiya Bukhari-Alston, Steve Rabinowitz and
The Libertarian Book Club, the Nicaragua Network, the
Village Voice's "Cheap Thrills" page (remember those insane
sixty to ninety-person tours from the early 1990s, where peo-
ple paid only $2.50 and complained about everything?), all of
the mainstream media that listed the tours—much to my surprise, Adriana Scopino for inviting me to speak in Union
Square in 1996 and introducing me to her publisher-husband
Dan Simon, and, last but not least, thousands of great political movements and hundreds of thousands of great people
who made a difference in the world. Where have you gone,
Emma Goldman and Abbie Hoffman?

INTRODUCTION

When I started Radical Walking Tours, on a rainy weekend in 1991 with nine people, I had no idea that all the sunny days I had spent at research in the library would lead to such success. Seven years later, after putting every free minute into the tours, I've a new appreciation for the small businessman. Radical Walking Tours grew out of almost twenty years of political activism and much reading. It seemed there wasn't a book I read on politics that didn't mention either a person or place related to New York City. Everyone from Fidel Castro to Leon Trotsky to John Reed to Abbie Hoffman has lived or worked in Manhattan. Unlike the Trumps and Rockefellers, however, there are few if any plaques of commemoration or buildings named in their honor: in the future, Trump Plaza will be Emma Goldman Plaza, serving as a free hotel for radicals in need of rest; Rockefeller Center will be a labor-organizing complex, and the Empire State Building will be a shelter for those in need of a home.

Until that day, however, I feel it's my duty to talk about a hidden history of the city.

Six years ago, a friend flattered me by seeing my work as important in that respect. She spent a year in Russia, and told of how previous sites of the Communist Regime were being replaced or covered with advertising billboards and other vulgar promotions for capitalism. Although Orwell's *1984* was about the Soviet Union, the parts about the Ministry of Information—the branch of totalitarian government responsible for changing history in books and magazines—are analogous to the United States today since a small number of corporations own the media and function similarly. How many times do we organize an important demonstration, only to watch the mainstream press, which reaches ninety percent of the population, entirely distort what happened or leave it out entirely, making it a non-event?

Another inspiration for the tours was to educate native New Yorkers and political organizers who walk by important sites every day and have no idea of their importance; in my experience, younger organizers don't tend to read the history of political movements to see what worked, what didn't, and why; it's my hope the tours inspire curiosity. Also, the '80s and '90s have been so difficult for organizing, and I want to inspire people to keep up the good fight by pointing out periods over the last two centuries when it's been less difficult, even thrilling. Finally, I've had a fascination with buildings or sites that are now decaying or ignored, and yet were the center of mass movements in previous eras. Like so many of the great political activists of the past, it's important that they too be remembered and respected.

I give about forty tours a year; to get a current schedule please call Radical Walking Tours at (718) 492-0069. The Web site is http://www.he.net/~radtours.

—Bruce Kayton
New York City
August 1998

NOTE: Each tour is arranged to correspond with the actual tours I give. They generally take a couple of hours to complete.

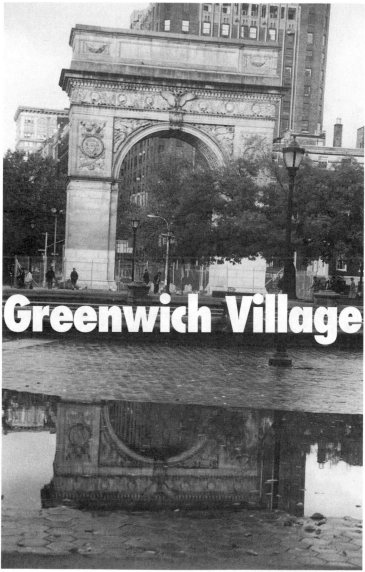

Greenwich Village

PHOTO BY MYRNA KAYTON

GREENWICH VILLAGE is one of the more serene and peaceful places to go, whether you're living in New York City or just passing through.

The Greenwich Village of legend is not really the same place today. Often, as I'm walking through The Village, someone with a tourist map in hand will ask, "Where is Greenwich Village?" I feel as though I'm lying when I tell them they are smack in the middle of it, since the Greenwich Village they are looking for doesn't exist anymore. They want to see bohemian-types engaged in counter-cultural activity, like John Reed running to a meeting of *The Masses*, or actors from the Provincetown Playhouse rehearsing an experimental play in a cafe, or a Woody Guthrie or young Bob Dylan strumming a guitar on a street-corner. *That* Greenwich Village doesn't exist anymore, and perhaps today only those with an income of the current Bob Dylan could afford to live in the Village.

The physicality of that era is gone too; many of the beautiful winding streets have been destroyed by the extension of Sixth and Seventh Avenues at the early part of the century and newer, more sterile-looking apartment buildings have replaced the beautiful three- or four-story nineteenth-century homes.

There's a famous story about anarchist waiter Hippolyte Havel who worked at Polly's Restaurant on MacDougal Street, who famously called the customers "Bourgeois Pigs." One day a customer asked him the boundaries of Greenwich Village. Hippolyte responded, "Greenwich Village is a state of mind; it has no boundaries." I hope the following tours take you to this state of mind.

GREENWICH VILLAGE I TOUR

❶ WASHINGTON SQUARE PARK—The Washington Square Arch (see photo on page 13) is a major symbol of Greenwich Village. The original was erected half a block north of its present location on the 100th anniversary of George Washington's taking the oath of office as the first president of the United States. It cost $2,756 (the current monthly rental price for a three-bedroom apartment in the area). It was built for the enjoyment of the rich living north of the park, not for the immigrants to the south. Local sugar merchant William Rhinelander Stewart was so impressed with it, and its potential to give a boost to local property values, that he raised $128,000 to build the current structure, completed in 1892. Atop the original arch was an all-black figure of George Washington, an irony considering the "Father of Our Country" lived on an estate built by slave labor, owned over three hundred slaves upon his death, and was even against letting Blacks fight in the American Revolution until there were major manpower shortages.

Since we're asked to remember Mr. Washington through countless statues, plaques, parks, and towns around the country named in his honor, let's remember also that at one point he was the richest person in the colonies and that his estate, along with those of the other founding fathers, was built by slaves who receive no such tribute. After he was dead, Mr. Washington exhibited great generosity toward the human

15

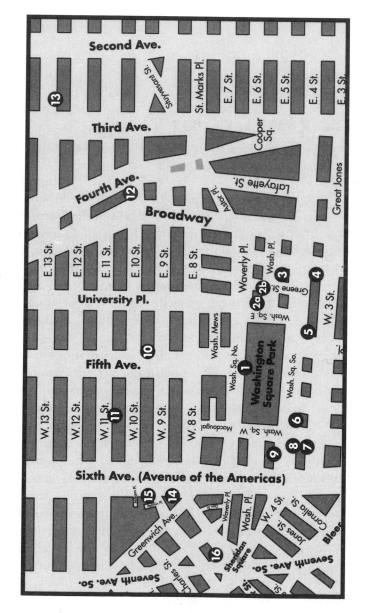

Greenwich Village I Tour

beings called his slaves: he gave a full one-third their freedom in his will.

There have been many symbolic take-overs of the arch throughout history. Probably the most famous was in 1917 when members of the bohemian Liberal Club climbed to the top and proclaimed "The Independent Republic of Greenwich Village." This crowd, known for carousing, included well-known artists John Sloane and Marcel Duchamp. The ceremony consisted of Greenwich Villager Gertrude Drick repeating the word "Whereas" over and over again. Though this was a very lighthearted take-over, another attempt to declare the Free Republic of Washington Square, this one in Central Park in 1913, was taken so seriously by the New York City Police Department that machine guns were set up and an arrest was made, though rains kept the crowds down and prevented further government violence.

Another famous take-over occurred in 1968. Organized by Students Against War and Racism, they barricaded themselves at the top during the Fifth Avenue Peace Parade against the Vietnam War. They flew a banner, along with the flag of the National Liberation Front of Vietnam, which read "The Streets Belong to the People."

Since the arch has been a symbol of freedom, always check the lock on the door at the side to see if fate will grant you a trip to the top.

Washington Square Park itself has a long and glorious history as a potter's field for those too poor to afford their burial; also a burial ground for Native Americans, African Americans (see Greenwich Village III Tour) and Germans. After a stint as a military parade ground, it became a park for good in the early 1850s and has a long history of the great spirit of public life, through numerous informal folksinging and comedy sessions, magic shows, walking tours, the dog run, and sports of all kinds happening simultaneously, blending peace and anarchy.

In the late 1950s, this urban oasis was threatened when the New York City Planning Commission decided to extend Fifth

Avenue through the park as a highway. Years of protest followed, led by a new magazine named *The Village Voice* and former first lady Eleanor Roosevelt. In 1963, the plan was defeated and a large party followed in celebration.

In 1961, when Robert Wagner was mayor, there were a series of protests over a curfew imposed on those "noisy, obnoxious...acoustic guitar-playing folksingers." Ten people were arrested and fifty others fled to the refuge of Judson Memorial Baptist Church south of the park. Future conservative Mayor Ed Koch was the lawyer representing the folksingers during this period; twenty-eight years later, as mayor, he imposed his own curfew in an attempt to keep the homeless out. Former Mayor Koch now lives in an apartment overlooking the park at 2 Fifth Avenue and presides over the moronic TV show "The People's Court."

Perhaps the best counter-cultural action was when the Yippies fought the restriction against leafletting in or within 150 feet of the park. In court, they won a suspension of the restriction, quickly running to the park with copies of the judgment, passing them out like leaflets. The police, unaware of the change in policy, arrested them for handing out copies of the judgment which stated they could no longer be arrested for handing out leaflets.

Many great protests ended in Washington Square Park, from anti-Gulf War demonstrations in the early 1990s to anti-curfew protests over Tompkins Square Park, as well as the Pot Parade, an annual event staged to protest the criminalization of marijuana.

②   a) NEW YORK UNIVERSITY (Main building, 100 Washington Square East)—New York University is the largest private university in the country, educating thirty-five thousand students who can manage the $23,000 annual tuition, room and board. They have tried to turn the Washington Square Park area into a local campus, and have taken over more buildings each year, forcing out older residents by raising rents, and knocking down some of those older buildings that gave Greenwich Village its reputation.

The first NYU building went up in 1835, and looked more like a gothic church than a university building. Prisoners in Sing-Sing Prison in Ossining, New York quarried the marble without any pay, but unionized stonecutters organized against the practice, which was getting more and more common. In 1834, they rioted in front of one of the contractor's buildings at 160 Broadway, causing $2,000 in damage and the intervention of the New York State National Guard. This was the first labor riot in New York State history and foreshadowed NYU's turbulent relations with its unions.

Struggles against the university continue and include demands for higher pay, the complaint of discrimination against African-American and Latino workers, and most recently the attempt to remove healthcare benefits.

NYU has assets totalling over $2 billion and remains a tax-free institution, even though it has investments in just about any industry you can name. They currently lease numbers One to Seven Washington Square North and as lessees, not owners, should not be entitled to tax exemptions. They are, however; a special tax exemption for NYU was passed in the New York State Legislature in 1984 that has cost the city over $8 million in lost revenue through 1992. The amount the taxpayers fund this private university keeps rising.

b) TRIANGLE SHIRTWAIST FACTORY FIRE OF 1911 (29 Washington Place, plaque on building corner at Greene Street)—One hundred forty-six workers, mostly young immigrant Jewish women, were killed in a flash fire in what was the largest sweatshop in New York City. The tragic deaths became a symbol of the horrible garment industry practices at that time. If it hadn't been a Saturday, when only half of the one thousand-person workforce was there, perhaps double the number would have perished.

The Triangle Shirtwaist Factory occupied the 8th, 9th and 10th floors of the building and as the fire spread dozens threw themselves from the windows, fearing death by incineration. Bodies were found piled up against doors that opened inward instead of outward; the only fire escape collapsed, and the fire department's hoses couldn't properly reach the top floors.

The owners of the factory escaped via the roof and lived to be acquitted in what was widely reported as a fixed, Tammany-Hall trial, involving bribes and perjured testimony. The owners were merely fined for piling sewing machines against an exit door. Five days after the tragedy, the factory moved to 5-11 University Place (where an NYU dormitory now stands).

Despite surviving a violent strike in 1909, the International Ladies Garment Workers Union (ILGWU) had not won full union rights at the shop. The owners had been fined many times for running an unsafe workplace, but there were few inspectors and the emphasis was on making the most shirtwaist dresses in the quickest time while taking up every available space with desks, sewing machines and piles of cloth. We like to think that those days are over, but in 1995 the General Accounting Office of the U.S. Government certified that New York City hosted forty-five hundred sweatshops employing fifty thousand people.

❸   ED KOCH'S RENT-CONTROLLED AND RENT-STABILIZED APARTMENT (14 Washington Place)—While Mayor, Ed Koch gave away hundreds of millions of dollars in tax breaks to the real estate industry to build luxury office and apartment houses. He was never worried about rent himself, however, since he lived in this apartment from the 1960s through 1989. Many of the luxury office buildings built in the 1980s are still empty. Mr. Koch's personal charisma and joke-telling ability endeared him to many middle-class New Yorkers, while his policies made it tougher for those trying to make ends meet. I'm often amazed when, on my tours, I talk about bombings, socialism, communism, and revolution no one has any objections until I criticize Ed Koch, apparently a folk hero to many people.

Walking down Greene Street, notice the restaurant on the corner of West Fourth Street (31 West Fourth St). It was the Campus Coffee Shop for over thirty years until 1993 when New York University forced them to close by increasing their rent by three hundred percent

4 **COURANT INSTITUTE/WARREN WEAVER HALL AT NYU (251 Mercer Street)**—Two hundred students occupied this building in May 1970 to protest NYU's ties to the then-named Atomic Energy Commission and held the $3.5 million computer hostage for a bargain price of $100,000 to raise bail for the Black Panthers for the "Panther 21" trial. The protest was part of the nationwide student strike against the Vietnam War and, more specifically, Nixon's "secret" bombing of Cambodia. When the NYU administration refused to budge, the anarchist group "Transcendental Students," wanted to use magnets to erase the information on the computer tapes, while the Marxists of Students for a Democratic Society (SDS) wanted to ignite Molotov cocktails and blow the computer up. SDS's plans won out, but the burning explosives were extinguished before any damage was done. Two professors who took part in the occupation were jailed, including Robert Wolfe, the current head of the Jewish Radical Education Project.

5 **ELMER HOLMES BOBST LIBRARY (70 Washington Square South)**—NYU has a great library which, outside of the important tenth floor, is open only to students and faculty. The tenth floor houses one of the best radical libraries in the country; open to the public, the Tamiment Institute Library is the place to go to see old copies of the *Jewish Daily Forward*, Emma Goldman's *Mother Earth* magazine, old socialist and communist leaflets and newspapers, as well as great union collections in the Robert F. Wagner Labor Archives. As I always talk about the immoral actions of people who have buildings named for them, I must point out that Elmer Holmes Bobst was a friend of former President Richard Nixon and was accused of sexually molesting his granddaughter.

6   ARTHUR T. VANDERBILT HALL, NYU (40 Washington Square South)—This block was owned by Papa Strunsky, who charged cheap rent in his aging apartment buildings and was extremely generous to the artists-tenants, letting rent slide if they needed it. The buildings were eventually knocked down after Columbia University sold the block to NYU in 1950 for $1 million. NYU erected the current Law School in 1951.

In 1911, a Harvard University graduate moved into an aging apartment building at what was then 42 Washington Square South. He shared the $30 per month rent with three roommates and went on to write *Ten Days That Shook the World, Insurgent Mexico,* and become one of the most famous political organizers in the United States. His name? John Reed, perhaps better known as the guy played by Warren Beatty in the movie *Reds* of the early 1980s.

7   POLLY'S RESTAURANT/PROVINCETOWN PLAYHOUSE (139/133 MacDougal Street)—Polly's Restaurant (in the basement next to 139 MacDougal Street) was run by an anarchist, Paula Holladay, in the 1910s. It hosted a whole cast of writers, poets, painters and radicals, including the members of the Liberal Club who climbed to the top of the Washington Square Arch. The previously mentioned Hippolyte Havel cooked and waited tables here, snarling at the middle-class customers, calling them "Bourgeois Pigs."

The Liberal Club was located above Polly's; it featured avant garde poetry readings, cubist art exhibitions, and one-act plays. Women did unheard-of things in front of the club like smoke and talk about free love and getting the right to vote. In 1914, a painting exhibition by the Liberal Club, featuring nudes, was shut down by the police.

129 MacDougal Street—former site of the lesbian bar of the 1920s that had a sign proclaiming, "Men are admitted but not welcome."
PHOTO BY BRUCE KAYTON

The Provincetown Playhouse was founded in Provincetown, Massachusetts in 1915, coming to the Village in 1916. It featured Eugene O'Neill, John Reed, Edna St. Vincent Millay, Max Eastman, and Louise Bryant (Reed's future wife). The Provincetown Playhouse staged experimental work, debuted Eugene O'Neill in America, and in an action unprecedented at that time, had African-American actors play African-American characters. The current Provincetown Playhouse is owned by the NYU Law Foundation. After sitting empty for several years, it reopened in 1998 with a play about the young Eugene O'Neill.

Note that the addresses of the above two sites are not the current ones; there were major renovations in the building in the 1940s and the numbering has changed.

This part of MacDougal Street was famous in the 1920s for its lesbian bar scene. The lesbian bar previously at 129 MacDougal Street had a clever sign out front to deal with the gender issue: "Men are admitted but not welcome." The three buildings at 127-131 MacDougal Street were all built for Aaron Burr in 1829.

Across the street from the Provincetown Playhouse is the west side of the NYU Law School, which covers the old site of Sam Schwartz's Speakeasy, one of many in the Village. This one is famous for having a waiter named Lee Chumley, who went on to start Chumley's on Bedford Street (See Greenwich Village II Tour).

Looking south down MacDougal, one can see the Minetta Tavern (113 MacDougal Street), where the late poet Allen Ginsberg had his first drink in the Village in the early 1940s.

At 119 MacDougal Street is the Cafe Reggio, featured prominently in the movie *Next Stop Greenwich Village*. It's the oldest continuously operating cafe in the Village, going back to 1927. In 1960, a young presidential candidate named John F. Kennedy made a campaign stop in front of the cafe.

❽   39 1/2 WASHINGTON SQUARE (entrance on West Fourth Street)—This beautiful building has enchanted me for years; I always had the feeling someone famous lived here. And, after years of giving tours, I discovered that Ida Rauh lived here, a trade-union organizer with the Women's Trade Union League who married future *Masses* magazine editor Max Eastman in 1911. Eastman hated the din from the street

The famous Cafe Reggio. PHOTO BY BRUCE KAYTON

39 1/2 Washington Square—former residence of Ida Rauh.
PHOTO BY BRUCE KAYTON

below, but liked the motto on Ida's wall—"Honesty, Simplicity, Intolerance."

❾ JOHN REED'S RENTAL APARTMENT (147 West Fourth Street)—The top floor of this house was where John Reed, in 1918, rented an apartment to get peace and quiet to finish writing *Ten Days That Shook the World*, the first detailed account of the Bolshevik take-over of Russia. His notes had been confiscated for months by U.S. Customs, and he feared his account would be stale if he didn't write it down immediately.

He began his classic account of the Russian Revolution at his Patchin Place apartment (See Site #15) and finished it here.

The main floor of this building housed another of Paula Holladay's restaurants.

❿ MABEL DODGE'S SALON (formerly at 23 Fifth Avenue)—The former building at this site was the Wednesday night meeting place for all of the Village bohemians in the 1910s, where artists and political radicals argued over topics like U.S. entry into WWI, free love versus marriage, and socialism versus anarchism.

Big Bill Haywood of the Industrial Workers of the World (IWW) came here to complain about the lack of publicity for the IWW-led Paterson, N.J. strike in 1913, leading John Reed and Mabel Dodge to join him in organizing the grand Paterson Pageant at Madison Square Garden (see the Chelsea-Ladies' Mile Tour).

This was believed to be the site where psychoanalysis (a radical concept at the time, though just as expensive as now) was first publicly discussed, and also where Emma Goldman taught Margaret Sanger about birth control, which led her to leave the socialist and labor movements to go full tilt into the birth control movement.

Ms. Dodge herself started the gatherings because she was

bored with her rich husband. She was famous in the Village as a nonjudgmental listener. She had a love affair with John Reed and later moved to Taos, New Mexico in 1918, setting up the twenty-two-room *Dodge Estate* which has housed over two dozen communes over time. It also served as the setting for the movie *Easy Rider* after actor Dennis Hopper bought it.

⑪ WEATHER UNDERGROUND TOWNHOUSE EX-PLOSION (18 West Eleventh Street)—On March 6, 1970, three members of the Weather Underground accidentally blew themselves up along with an 1840s townhouse that was on sale for $255,000. The Weather Underground was a militant splinter group of Students for a Democratic Society. They were tired of both being beaten up by police at demonstrations and of listening to politicians' speeches while millions died in Vietnam. They saw the United States Empire increasing its power and decided it was time to fight fire with fire. They organized violent demonstrations, invaded high schools and beaches and decided to stage a series of symbolic bombings against state and corporate targets.

The bomb killed Ted Gold, Diana Oughton and Terry Robbins. Kathy Boudin and Cathy Wilkerson, whose parents owned the home and were away for the summer, ran out naked to the house next door (#16—Dustin Hoffman's house). After getting some clothing from Hoffman's wife, they disappeared into the subway and remained underground for many years. Cathy Wilkerson eventually turned herself in and received a light sentence. Kathy Boudin was later arrested for being part of the Black Liberation Army appropriation of a Brink's truck in Nyack, New York in 1981, for which she received a stiff jail sentence.

The current building, markedly different from the others in the row, was built in 1978 and serves as an unofficial memorial to those who died fighting for a better world.

The Weather Underground explosion on March 6, 1970 accounts for this contemporary building amongst older brownstones on Eleventh Street near Fifth Avenue. PHOTO BY PETER JOSEPH

⑫ THE BREADLINES AND FLEISCHMANN'S MODEL VIENNA BAKERY (this site adjoins Grace Church on Tenth Street between Broadway and Fourth Avenue)—The famous bakery was in business from 1876 to 1909 on the site where the playground now stands. In the 1880s, in order to prove how fresh its products were, it gave out unsold items at midnight, free of charge, to the unemployed or homeless. The lines that formed for blocks popularized the term "breadlines." That horrible tradition continues to this day in New York City. In one of the richest cities in the history of the world, dozens of soup kitchens operate to feed those for whom capitalism is unable to provide.

As one walks to Emma Goldman's house (see below) one is entering the East Village—going slightly beyond the boundaries of a Greenwich Village tour. (At the time I wrote this tour, I had no idea I would write a dozen more, and that Emma should have been placed in one of the East Village tours, so I apologize for this extra walking, but I'm sure Emma would have wanted you to go that extra distance to see her home. More likely she would have screamed at me for leading a tour instead of a demonstration.)

⑬ EMMA GOLDMAN'S HOUSE (208 East Thirteenth Street, formerly 210 East Thirteenth Street)—Emma Goldman, one of the most inspiring, anti-authoritarian, anti-rich, anti-military activists who ever lived, resided in this building from 1903 to 1913. Radical Walking Tours placed a plaque here on the first floor in 1995 to commemorate her life. Emma's life here represented one of her longest stretches of staying out of jail, a place with which she became familiar, usually for doing no more than speaking—so much for the proud history of the First Amendment.

She was arrested in Union Square for speaking about birth control, arrested in Manhattan for forming an anti-draft organization in World War I, deported to the Soviet Union for being an anarchist, was the first anarchist in the United States to go on a coast-to-coast speaking tour and was an outspoken supporter of the Spanish Revolution in the 1920s. She published *Mother Earth* magazine from here and later wrote one of the most inspiring books of the century, *Living My Life*, her two-volume autobiography, still in print (published by Dover).

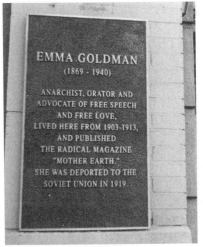

The plaque placed by Radical Walking Tours on Emma Goldman's 1903–1913 residence. PHOTO BY MYRNA KAYTON

As you walk back towards Sixth Avenue, note the Strand Book Store on the corner of Broadway and Twelfth Street, one of the best used bookstores in NYC. Don't go in unless you have money and a short trip home because you'll be carrying a lot of books. Someone once said that used bookstores are the equivalent of the lottery for intellectuals. In The Strand, you're likely to find that one gem that's eluded you.

14 JEFFERSON MARKET LIBRARY AND SITE OF FORMER WOMEN'S HOUSE OF DETENTION (425 Sixth Avenue at Tenth Street)—The current library was famous earlier in the century as the Jefferson Market Courthouse, where the picketing strikers at the Triangle Shirtwaist Factory were arraigned during the 1909 "Uprising of the 20,000" in the garment industry. There was a jail behind it, later to become the Women's House of Detention, and now a garden. It's twelve stories did not quite fit into Greenwich Village, it being unusual enough for a jail to be located within the heart of a community; it made for many demonstrations on behalf

The Jefferson Market Library viewed from the rear. Where there are now trees was once the site of a women's prison. PHOTO BY PETER JOSEPH

of those inside. While noting the many famous people who spent time behind bars, one shouldn't forget all of the anonymous women who spent time here, including those who were heavily drugged on the fourth floor psychiatric wing.

In 1950, Mrs. Griselio Torresola was held here following the death of her husband on November 1, 1950, after an attempted assassination of President Truman in Blair House in Washington, D.C. in support of the Puerto Rican Independence Movement. Though this attack shocked the nation and was widely denounced, it was done to avenge the suppression of a nationalist rebellion in Puerto Rico where twenty-five Puerto Ricans were killed and many more injured by the occupying forces.

In 1957, Catholic Worker founder Dorothy Day (see East Village II Tour) was jailed here for protesting with the War Resister's League against air raid drills and the Cold War at City Hall. In the early 1960s, Judith Malina, founder of the Living Theater, and notorious feminist Andrea Dworkin were imprisoned here for an anti-Vietnam War protest. They got the then-liberal *New York Post* to do a photo exposé on the horrible prison conditions.

Also in the 1950s, alleged Soviet spy Ethel Rosenberg (see Lower East Side I Tour) was jailed here twice, her beautiful singing voice filling the entire jail. If one looks down Sixth Avenue to the north entrance of the West Fourth Street Station just below Eighth Street, you will see where her frightened husband Julius Rosenberg met with his future lawyer, Emmanuel Bloch, after receiving a visit from the FBI in 1950.

In 1970, perhaps the most famous resident of this jail was Angela Davis, held for two months after being captured at an uptown Howard Johnson's Hotel. As an African-American Communist Party Professor with a large Afro, she was J. Edgar Hoover's biggest nightmare. She was charged with aiding Jonathan Jackson, the brother of her lover George Jackson, in an attempted courthouse escape in Marin County, California.

On December 20, 1970, she was taken out of the jail at 3:00 AM, driven through an emptied and cleared Holland Tunnel, and flown to California where, after almost a year in jail and a court case of ninety-five witnesses and two hundred exhibits, she was acquitted of all charges by an all-white jury.

In 1971, there were protests on behalf of two of the female members of the "Panther 21" held inside. The "Panther 21" were charged with conspiracy, but were acquitted on all charges after an eight-month trial and three hours of jury deliberation.

The Women's House of Detention was closed in 1971; the women were moved to Riker's Island, far from where it's easy for activists to cause trouble. The building, erected in 1931, was demolished in 1973-1974 and replaced by the current garden, run by volunteers from the community.

Before the Women's House of Detention, there was a co-ed jail here which held Mae West after her "lascivious" plays of the 1920s. In 1906, it held Harry K. Thaw, the deranged Pittsburgh capitalist who murdered architect Stanford White on the roof of the old Madison Square Garden (see Chelsea-Ladies' Mile Tour).

⑮ PATCHIN PLACE (Small alley on Tenth Street between Greenwich Avenue and Sixth Avenue)—This beautiful enclave was built in the 1840s as workers' quarters for the Hotel Brevoort on Fifth Avenue (see Greenwich Village III Tour). It has become a very expensive and desirable Village residence. Number One is the apartment which Louise Bryant (John Reed's wife) kept so she could maintain a residence in

Number One Patchin Place—once home to Louise Bryant.
PHOTO BY BRUCE KAYTON

the United States and be allowed to return to the U.S. after her trip to the Soviet Union. John Reed started writing *Ten Days That Shook the World* here, only to move to a West Fourth Street apartment (see above, #9) due to interruptions.

Louise Bryant also wrote a great book on the emerging Soviet Union. She was almost prevented from returning to the U.S. from the Soviet Union when a telegram from the U.S. government, telling officials to detain her, arrived one day after she left.

Six Patchin Place was John Howard Lawson's residence for sixteen years (see Greenwich Village II Tour). He spent a year in jail for contempt as a member of the "Hollywood Ten" during the McCarthy Era, a time of tremendous conformity when the current term "politically correct" should really have been coined.

Milligan Place, adjacent to Patchin Place, is accessible around the corner on Sixth Avenue; its residents have included Provincetown Playhouse founders George Cram Cook and Susan Glaspell as well as playwright Eugene O'Neill.

⑯   STONEWALL INN (53 Christopher Street)—This converted barn, then third-rate bar, became a worldwide symbol of the modern gay rights movement in June 1969 after patrons of the bar fought back against a police raid. Over a two-night period, gay men threw everything they could grab against the arresting officers and even trapped several officers inside before the front glass window was broken and the Tactical Police Force was sent in.

Years of pent-up fury over harassment of the gay and lesbian community was released during this police raid. Gay and lesbian groups and newspapers sprang up around the country and around the world, powered by the energy of the Civil Rights, Feminist and Anti-Vietnam War Movements. Craig Rodwell, who ran the Oscar Wilde Memorial Bookshop down the block (see Greenwich Village II Tour), quickly organized against the police.

The legendary Stonewall Inn, site of the great uprising that became a benchmark in the gay rights movement. PHOTO BY BRUCE KAYTON

Through his efforts, and those of other early gay rights activists, we now have the Gay Pride March, which has unfortunately become more of a party than a political event.

Note the street signs on the corners, delineating that part of the street as Stonewall Place. In the '80s, then-Mayor Ed Koch presided over the official renaming of the area and was justifiably booed by local residents for his inaction on the AIDS issue and lack of support of gay rights.

Greenwich Village II Tour

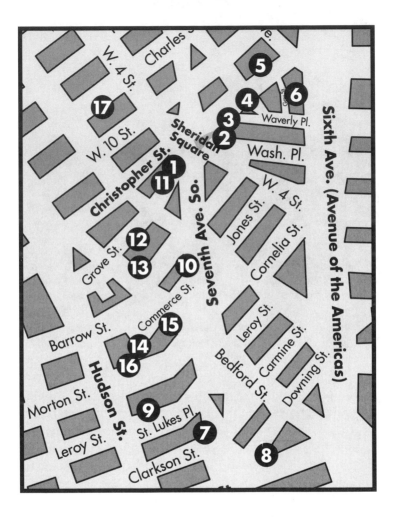

GREENWICH VILLAGE II TOUR

❶ SHERIDAN SQUARE—This square represents the more commercial side of Greenwich Village as evidenced by the large number of tourist traps in the area. This tradition goes back to the late 1910s, when the radicals and bohemians were chased out of Greenwich Village by imitation bohemian restaurants which co-opted their culture. There were theme restaurants like the Toby Club with fake spiders and spiderwebs, the Pirates' Den where waiters and waitresses got into swordfights, and other clubs imitating prisons, farms and Native American lifestyles.

Such places thrived into the 1920s, as prohibition went into effect. Around that time, there was a tremendous fear of not being able to get a drink for the rest of one's life; it proved short-lived however, as, according to Police Commissioner Grover Whalen, the number of speakeasies in New York City, from 1919-1933, doubled from fifteen to thirty thousand. The police would even help you start your own liquor club, in return for a percentage of the profits.

At 5 Sheridan Square, in a building that's been replaced by the current apartment building at 3 Sheridan Square, Barney Gallant ran the Greenwich Village Inn, where he refused to stop serving liquor. When the police tried to arrest one of his waiters for serving liquor, he intervened and had himself arrested, saying he was the architect of the operation. He got a thirty-day sentence in the Tombs, but his arrest was so strongly supported by his fans—and he had many in the

Village—that he had a waiting list of visitors, which embarrassed the authorities.

In true "Village Spirit," when the government tried to release him early he refused to leave because he enjoyed the publicity.

The famous Village Independent Democratic Club was located on the second floor at 224 West Fourth Street. It was a voice of liberalism in the 1950s and 1960s, with the likes of Ed Koch, before he became a corporate puppet, and the late Bella Abzug. This site housed the Greenwich Village Theater, where Eugene O'Neill had his plays produced after he outgrew the Provincetown Playhouse.

Other famous sites around the square include 1 Sheridan Square, the former site of Cafe Society, later Charles Ludlam's Ridiculous Theatrical Company. At Cafe Society, in 1961, a benefit concert was given by local folksingers to honor one of America's greatest folksingers—Woody Guthrie.

One hundred-one Seventh Avenue South was a famous lesbian bar called the Duchess, until then-Mayor Ed Koch took its liquor license away in the '80s by using the anti-discrimination laws against it, effectively closing it down.

Sheridan Square is named for Philip Sheridan, whose statue from the 1930s adorns Christopher Park. Like most of the people honored in this city through statues, he was a man who murdered people, serving as a Civil War general for the North. He's most famous for his statement that "The only good Indian is a dead Indian."

❷   88 GROVE STREET—This was Rose Pastor Stokes' home in 1918. She was a Socialist, birth control activist, and one of the founders of the American Communist Party, who deserves more fame than she has received.

She was arrested here for voting, and arraigned at the Jefferson Market Courthouse on Sixth Avenue. She was first arrested for writing a letter to a Kansas newspaper opposing U.S. entry into WWI and was out on $10,000 bail, so when she voted she was technically a convicted felon under the Espionage Act, which makes one ineligible to vote (New York women won the right to vote in 1918 thanks to a 1917 city-wide referendum and strong Socialist Party support through mayoral candidate Morris Hillquit's campaign). Eventually, the ridiculous charges were dropped. (For more on Rose Pastor Stokes, see the Lower East Side I Tour.)

3   **92 GROVE STREET**—This was the site where African Americans were given refuge during the Draft Riots of July 1863. During the heart of the Civil War, working-class men rioted for four days, protesting the national draft. The city government was almost overthrown, barricades a mile long went up on the west side, draft offices were destroyed, and troops on their way to fight confederate troops were diverted to New York City. Sheridan Square was the scene of some of the riots.

The working class fought for two divergent reasons: 1) Resentment over the fact that the rich could buy their way out of the draft for $300 and 2) Racism caused them to blame African Americans for the war, and so they became a target of the violence.

It is estimated that at least fifty thousand people rioted; a small percent of the African-American population of Manhattan moved out after being terrorized. The only major hospital to give African Americans refuge was the Jews Hospital, on West Twenty-eighth Street, which later changed its name to Mt. Sinai Hospital and moved uptown.

4   **NORTHERN DISPENSARY (165 Waverly Place)**—This landmark went up in 1831, serving the medical needs of the poor. A $3 annual donation allowed a donor to send one of his servants for free. After 1960, it became a dental clinic. Folksinger Harry Chapin used it as a child. In 1986, George Whitmore, a patient at the clinic, disclosed that he had AIDS and the clinic refused to treat him. He sued through the Human Rights Commission and won a $46,000 judgment,

The Northern Dispensary—once an inexpensive medical, then dental clinic.
PHOTO BY PETER JOSEPH

which caused the clinic to go bankrupt and it's been empty ever since.

However, in a move proving there can be justice in the world, it is soon to become a permanent housing facility for people with AIDS, despite the opposition of local residents. On the next block, at the corner of Waverly Place and Tenth Street, there was a horrible gay-bashing incident in 1993; two men holding hands were attacked by three men with golf clubs, fracturing the skull of one of the victims. Appallingly low bail was set after the arrest of the attackers, and a very lenient plea bargain was withdrawn after the case was publicized by the community.

Though we think of New York City, especially Greenwich

Village, as a place of tolerance, there are many incidents of violence on gays and lesbians, particularly on weekends.

5 **OSCAR WILDE MEMORIAL BOOKSHOP (15 Christopher Street)**—This is the oldest storefront gay and lesbian bookstore in the world, started by gay rights activist Craig Rodwell in 1967 on Mercer Street. Craig was extremely active after the Stonewall Riots and, until his death in 1993, he very bravely maintained this store, standing up to death threats and broken windows. The bookstore has a great collection of books, magazines, video and audio cassettes, and buttons. It is named for Irish playwright Oscar Wilde who was jailed for being gay; in his court trial, he talked about homosexuality as "the love that dare not speak its name."

6 **LAW PRACTICE OF THE LATE WILLIAM KUNSTLER AND EX-PARTNER RON KUBY (13 Gay Street)**—This house is the site made famous through all of the work these two radical attorneys did over the years. The practice continues, though at a different address after the death of

The famous Oscar Wilde Memorial Bookshop on Christopher Street.
PHOTO BY PETER JOSEPH

Bill in 1995, when Kuby had a dispute with his widow, Margaret Ratner.

Gay Street is not named for the large gay population living here but for an old Dutch family. This beautiful winding street was also an African-American neighborhood in the 1840s, where many servants working in the area lived. Prior to the Civil War one-quarter of New York City's African-American population lived on Bleecker, Thompson, Sullivan, and MacDougal Streets.

7   CARMINE RECREATION CENTER (Corner of Clarkson and Varick Streets)—This public center was erected in 1908 and holds two of the fifty-six city pools open to the public, either for free or at a very low cost. More importantly, it sits on the site of the Clarkson Street Men's Association, founded in 1830.

In July 1863, shortly after midnight during the first day of the Draft Riots, an African-American man was dragged from the club and lynched. The racist murderers danced a jig under the body.

Down the block at 21 Seventh Avenue South is Nanny's, the famous lesbian bar, which on the Sunday night of the Gay Pride March has its sidewalk overflowing with joyous women.

8   DOWNING STREET—This is one of the few streets in New York City originally named for an African American. The Downing family was prominent in eightenth- and early nineteenth-century New York. They owned restaurants throughout Manhattan, one of which served as a stop on the underground railroad for escaped slaves (see the Wall Street Tour).

George Downing was a founding member of the African Free Schools in 1787, which gave a free education to African Americans as slavery was being outlawed in New York State. There were over a dozen of these schools in lower Manhattan, and they served over five thousand people, including one thousand children. They were originally run by the Manumission Society, eventually merging with the public school system.

9   6 ST. LUKES PLACE—This address in a row of fifteen three-story rowhouses went up in the 1850s and was where Jimmy Walker grew up and later lived during his reign as mayor of New York City (one and three-quarter terms in the late 1920s and early 1930s). Mr. Walker's mayoralty foreshadowed the modern politician, forever untarnished in scandal after scandal.

He did very little work, and was notorious for being loved by the press and taking constant vacations. He used to brag that he never read a newspaper or answered a constituent's letter. His good looks, dancing, and songwriting abilities made him a symbol of the Roaring Twenties. He was finally forced to resign in 1932, and was divorced in 1941 by the mistress he had married. The house was sold for nonpayment of taxes.

The block is one of the most beautiful in the Village and the rowhouses contain much history. Number Ten served as the exterior of Bill Cosby's home in the famous 1980s sitcom *The Cosby Show*; I'm sure the network didn't realize they shot next door to Max Eastman's old residence, which was raided by the police in 1920 (Number 11—see Greenwich Village III Tour), and again in 1965, when Timothy Leary and Dick Alpert used to live there. Number Sixteen was where Communist Party supporter Theodore Dreiser wrote *An American Tragedy* and Number Twelve housed Sherwood Anderson, some of whose stories from *Winesburg, Ohio* were first published in *The Masses* (see Greenwich Village III).

Across the street, where the softball field now stands, was the Trinity Parish Cemetery in which nineteenth-century writer Edgar Allen Poe would wander.

The large wail separating the softball field from the outdoor pool displays a vast Keith Haring mural. Haring started as a graffiti artist and soon was painting murals for just about every political benefit of the late 1980s, including Nelson Mandela's birthday celebration in England. He died in 1990, but his work continues to live through The Pop Shop at 292 Lafayette Street in Soho.

⑩   9 COMMERCE STREET (at Seventh Avenue South)—If this building looks as if someone literally cut a piece off, it's because they did. In the 1910s, it was decided to extend the Seventh Avenue subway line below Fourteenth Street to Houston Street. It was also decided, by fiat, that since the subway was to be extended, so too was Seventh Avenue to create what is now Seventh Avenue South. All the buildings in the way were to be knocked down.

The row of houses on Commerce Street begins at number nine because numbers one, three, five and seven were where Seventh Avenue South now plows through. This major construction project, from 1911 to 1917, cleared 194 buildings, and destroyed many of the old winding streets. Village radicals of the bohemian era credit this construction with the death of the bohemian era, since the Village was made to look more like the standard 'avenued' neighborhoods, allowing car culture to invade, making the area easily accessible to tourists.

You can see the weird triangular formations created by the construction of Seventh Avenue South, many of which became gas stations and auto supply shops. The small shops that filled up these empty triangles became known as "taxpayers," because their rent to the landlord of the square block would pay off the real estate taxes on the property.

⑪   MARIE'S CRISIS CAFE (59 Grove Street)—This restaurant and piano bar commemorates the site where the eventually spurned American revolutionary, Thomas Paine, died in 1809. The current building went up in 1839 and is named for Mr. Paine's *Crisis Papers*, which began with the famous line "These are the times that try men's souls." Though famous throughout the world, Mr. Paine grew less popular for his opposition to organized religion. He had a nasty exchange of letters with George Washington when he was jailed in France for his politics in 1793, and the Father of our Country refused to help free him.

⑫ EMMA GOLDMAN'S LAST RESIDENCE IN THE UNITED STATES (36 Grove Street)

Emma Goldman lived here in 1919, before she was deported to the Soviet Union via Finland from Ellis Island. Her comrade and fellow deportee, Alexander Berkman, organized the sailors on the boat, the SS Buford, that was deporting them. They offered to turn around and take him back, but Berkman turned down their offer because he wanted to work for the new Bolshevik Regime in the Soviet Union.

Plaque in front of Marie's Crisis Cafe on Grove Street, commemorating the fact that Tom Paine died there.
PHOTO BY PETER JOSEPH

Emma and Alexander set up the Museum of the Revolution in the Soviet Union, but eventually turned against the repressive policies of the Bolsheviks and left the country a couple of years later. Down the block, at 45 Grove Street, is the last manor house left in the Village. It was the residence of famous gay poet Hart Crane, and served as the house of Eugene O'Neill (played by Jack Nicholson) in the movie *Reds*.

⑬ CHUMLEY'S (86 Bedford Street)

This well-known unmarked restaurant is famous for being a speakeasy during Prohibition. It's little-known, however, for its more radical past. Owner Lee Chumley published the local Industrial Workers of the World's newspaper here, and held secret meetings in the 1920s. The Industrial Workers of the World (IWW) was one of the leading radical movements of the 1910s, made famous for its songwriting, organizing, fighting free speech fights on street corners, and being deported and killed during various actions on the east and west coasts.

The building itself has many entrances, including an alleged underground tunnel that leads one block away.

Police raids during the Prohibition Era for illegal liquor produced no arrests, but once Lee Chumley was arrested in a political raid, for the crime of having an illegal pen knife. More importantly, his typewriter was confiscated when the police couldn't charge him with anything more serious than possessing the knife.

⑭   CHERRY LANE THEATER (38 Commerce Street)— This building was originally a brewery when it went up in 1836, but in the 1920s it served as the home of the New Playwrights Theater, featuring the work of Michael Gold, John Dos Passos, and John Howard Lawson, who became famous for being fired as a screenwriter by the movie studios in the 1930s for supporting Upton Sinclair's socialist California gubernatorial campaign. He also served a year in jail as a member of the "Hollywood Ten" during the 1950s McCarthy Era (see Greenwich Village I Tour).

In 1924, Edna St. Vincent Millay, noted Village playwright, poet, and actress, moved the Provincetown Playhouse here because she felt the productions were getting too commercial. In 1951, the theater served as the first permanent home of the anarchist "Living Theater," led by Judith Malina and Julian Beck. They were arrested all over the world for their political and revolutionary productions, including *The Brig* in the early 1960s, a play about Marine boot camps.

The Living Theater currently has no official home, but has been doing excellent street theater against the death penalty around New York City.

The bend in Commerce Street, just past the theater, follows the curve of Dutch Governor Wouter Van Twiller's farm in the 1630s. He was famous for taking over land with his gubernatorial privileges; he also had a tobacco farm in what is now the northwest part of Washington Square Park.

⑮   77 BEDFORD STREET—This building goes back to 1799 and is considered the oldest house in the Village, though it's had two major alterations. The first owner, Harmon Hendricks, had the first copper rolling plant in the American colonies; he and Paul Revere cornered the market in Colonial America, providing almost all the copper broilers used to make rum. I always felt that Paul Revere's famous ride should have carried the cry "The British are coming; The British are coming and they're going to take my copper monopoly away!" This would provide a more accurate description of what the American Revolution was fought over.

Next door is 75 1/2 Bedford Street, known as the narrowest house in the Village. It was built originally as a carriage entrance for the bigger house next door and at nine and one-half by thirty-five feet is now a desired residence in "Always a Housing Shortage and Kept That Way by the Landlords" New York City. Edna St. Vincent Millay lived here for a year in the 1920s while married to Max Eastman's old roommate, Eugen Bossevain. Archie Leach, better known later as Cary Grant, also lived here with his male lover, but they had to get a third roommate to make the $15 per month rent.

The building sold for $270,000 in 1993 and currently rents for, according to *The New York Times*, $6,000 per month.

⑯ ALLEGED ROSENBERG ESPIONAGE APARTMENT (65 Morton Street)—Apartment 6I was alleged by the FBI to be a "spy den," used by Julius and Ethel Rosenberg in the 1940s (when the Soviet Union and United States were allies). On June 19, 1953, the height of the cold war, the Rosenbergs were executed in Sing-Sing prison for stealing the secret of the atomic bomb, though it was not quite a secret at the time.

⑰ 74 CHARLES STREET—The fourth-floor walk-up in this building was home to Communist Party member and one of America's most famous folksingers, Woody Guthrie, in the early 1940s. Woody Guthrie paid $27 per month in rent for what was then a dusty and dingy apartment as he waited for the

Julius'—still standing at Tenth and Waverly. Woody Guthrie drank here.
PHOTO BY PETER JOSEPH

love of his life. Marjorie Mazia, to divorce her husband and move in with him.

Guthrie spent a lot of time in Greenwich Village. He set up *Almanac House*, a folksinging commune, on Greenwich Avenue and Tenth Street with Pete Seeger. He drank at the White Horse Tavern on Hudson Street and Julius' on Tenth Street and Waverly Place. He played his guitar in Washington Square Park with Rambling Jack Elliot in the 1950s, and was widely idolized (and copied) by everyone from Bob Dylan to Phil Ochs. His most famous song is *This Land is Your Land*, a tribute to the average American in which the most radical verse about private property is usually dropped.

Woody died in 1967, as the folksinging movement he helped popularize was in revival, living long enough, however, to see his son Arlo record *Alice's Restaurant Massacre*.

I would end this tour closer to the river on Charles and West Streets where the Pathfinder Mural was displayed from 1989 to 1996. This 5,950 square-foot mural of radicals took two-and-a-half years to complete and featured the work of eighty artists from twenty countries. Featured radicals included Maurice Bishop, Karl Marx, Leon Trotsky, and Nelson Mandela; it was unfortunately taken down due to deterioration.

The Socialist Workers Party's Pathfinder Press building, (which had the mural on its south wall), still exists at 14 Charles Lane, from where *The Militant* newspaper is published.

GREENWICH VILLAGE III TOUR

1 **WASHINGTON SQUARE PARK (African-American History)**—Though predominantly white, Greenwich Village wasn't always that way (see Greenwich Village II Tour—Gay Street). In the seventeenth century, when the Dutch set up New Amsterdam, they used over three hundred slaves—out of a total population of fifteen hundred—to do all the essential labor in the new colony.

Slavery started in New Amsterdam in the mid-1620s, when the first eleven male slaves, pirated from a Portuguese vessel, arrived; some of their names were Paul D'Angola, Simon Congo, John Francisco, and Big and Little Manuel. The Dutch were less vicious than the British in their slave-owning practices; they allowed Africans to testify in court, own property, and legally marry. They also promised the first African slaves their freedom after between ten to forty years of servitude (how generous).

These first slaves were given land and freedom in a series of thirty grants from 1635 to 1665, totalling one hundred-fifty to two hundred acres, including the Washington Square Park area with plots extending to Astor Place on the east side, Union Square to the north, and Sixth Avenue on the west. Eventually, all of the land was either taken back or bought back by whites, as there were several loopholes in the original grants.

2 **JUDSON MEMORIAL BAPTIST CHURCH (55 Washington Square South)**—Founded in 1891 by Edward

Greenwich Village III Tour

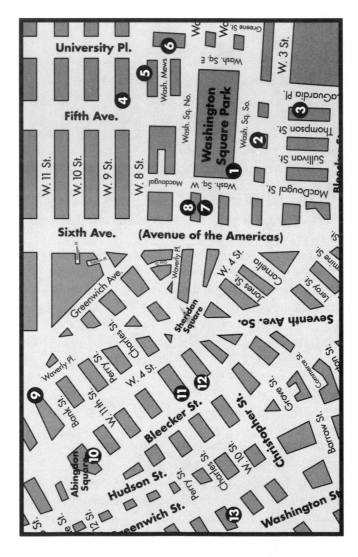

Judson, the church was designed by architect Stanford White. It served, at the turn of the century, as a headquarters for social work, before the institutionalization of the profession. The church got immigrants jobs, provided healthcare, took

The Judson Memorial Baptist Church on Washington Square.
PHOTO BY PETER JOSEPH

care of immigrant children, and tried to get donations from the rich living north of the park to help the immigrants living south of the park.

In the 1950s, Bob Spike, a civil rights activist, led the church in establishing political art exhibits, and strengthening the notion that since it exists for the community, no issue is too controversial for church involvement. That philosophy continued under Reverend Howard Moody; the church was the first in the area to establish a drug treatment clinic in 1961.

The following year the Hall of Issues began, a tradition wherein anyone can put up their own artwork Sundays from 2:00 to 5:00 PM.

During the Folksinger Riots of 1961 (see Greenwich Village I Tour) the church provided refuge for those fleeing the police.

In 1965, Bob Nichols, an activist, went on a hunger strike for over a week from a couch in the church to protest President Johnson's ever-escalating Vietnam War, prompting a letter from the Department of Defense; they were worried about his health—and, no doubt, the possibility of negative publicity should he get seriously ill.

In 1967, the church openly made referrals to women for then-illegal abortions and, despite a front page article in *The New York Times*, they were never shut down.

In the mid-1960s, Police Chief Stanford Garelick spoke at a community forum on the entrapment of gay men at bars in the Village and Times Square area. He said he would put a stop to such harassment, but there were actually arrests at gay bars the very night of the forum, proving his admonition, that gay men report any raids to the police, was disingenuous. Reverend Moody testified in the City Council on behalf of the Gay and Lesbian Rights Bill each year, and included his church in the march in the Gay Pride Parade each year.

In 1992, the AIDS Coalition To Unleash Power (ACT-UP) took part in an open-casket funeral march which started at the church. Thirty-eight-year-old activist-architect Mark

Fisher wanted to demonstrate, with his body, the "criminal neglect" of the government that facilitated the spread of AIDS. The funeral, which took place in the rain, was inspired by the many South African funerals by anti-apartheid activists. The body was carried to President George Bush's presidential re-election headquarters on West Forty-third Street, where the Yuppies inside stood aghast.

In 1970, the church put on its famous flag show, where everything imaginable was made using the design of the flag—Abbie Hoffman's shirt, bras, cakes, coffins, dolls, etc. It was shut down by the police after three days.

In the late 1970s, Reverend Moody and his assistant, the late Arlene Carman, worked with prostitutes, setting up a hospitality van, and providing healthcare referrals—they eventually wrote a book about their experiences (*Working Women: The Subterranean World of Street Prostitution*). They felt the church shouldn't judge the prostitutes, but instead improve their working conditions. Arlene was mistakenly arrested for solicitation one night on Eight Avenue and won a $6,000-$7,000 settlement, further empowering the women.

The church's bulletin board has always had political quotations on it, and during the Vietnam War kept a bodycount of those killed both in combat and at home, like Black Panthers and students. When President Ronald Reagan went to pay homage to the Nazi cemetery in Bitburg, Germany in the mid-1980s, the message on the bulletin board exclaimed, "For God's sake, Mr. President, Never Again Means Never Again."

The church recently completed a renovation, and continues to be a beautiful Greenwich Village landmark. For years, NYU has wanted to take it over—they do own the section west of the tower, which was a hotel—and yet the church remains a beacon of service to the people.

❸ LOEB STUDENT CENTER (NYU: 566-576 LaGuardia Place)—This building went up in 1959 and, contrary to NYU's wishes, served as the school's command post for the national student strike that began after President Nixon's invasion of Cambodia during the Vietnam War. Several students returned from a Black Panther rally in New Haven, Connecticut and presented three demands, as part of a call for a national student strike. The NYU students approved a call for a student strike and the last three weeks of classes were cancelled.

When school resumed in the fall, activists have said, it was like re-inventing the wheel in organizing because the summer break de-politicized the campus.

In 1968, the South Vietnamese Ambassador to the U.S. tried to speak to a gathering of the Young Republicans, but was prevented by local activists who lowered the South Vietnamese flag and raised the flag of the National Liberation Front. Tom Wicker of *The New York Times* also had a talk disrupted at the center, an action widely criticized on free speech grounds.

Also in 1968, an overflow crowed paid tribute to slain Civil Rights Leader Martin Luther King, Jr.

In the 1980s, veteran Yippie pie thrower Aaron Kaye hit hydrogen bomb creator Edward Teller with, appropriately, a mushroom pie.

4   SITE OF THE OLD BREVOORT HOTEL (Formerly 15 Fifth Avenue, currently the Brevoort Apartments)—The old hotel opened in 1854 and housed many people over the years during its nearly century-long existence: Eugene O'Neill, Lincoln Steffens, Theodore Drciscr, Isadora Duncan, and Edna St. Vincent Millay.

Its cafe was a famous hangout for the "Village Crowd," and cases upon cases of whiskey were given away on the night of June 30, 1919, the first day of Prohibition. A massive panic swept the country; the fear that alcohol would be a thing of the past. The fear proved short-lived, even though the cafe was padlocked in 1926 for violating prohibition, illegal liquor flowed during Prohibition, particularly in the Village.

Its radical history began in 1915, when a dinner was held

in honor of birth-control activist Margaret Sanger, facing trial after fleeing to Europe for a year for putting out an eight-page birth control newspaper called *The Woman Rebel*. Sanger wrote about how people were going to use birth control whether the government approved or not and that it was a choice between having available birth control or infanticide and abortion. The charges against Sanger were dropped (see the Chelsea–Ladies' Mile Tour).

That same year, on the eve of Emma Goldman's trial for publicly explaining how to use a contraceptive, a banquet was held in her honor here. Rose Pastor Stokes handed out type-written sheets with information on birth control, and the next day Emma served as her own lawyer in court. The judge ended up sentencing her to fifteen days in jail or a $100 fine and since Emma was morally opposed to paying a fine to the government, she served the time in the Queens County Jail.

In 1919, the Brevoort Hotel was one of the few venues in New York City willing to host a reception dinner for Emma Goldman and Alexander Berkman on the eve of their deportation from the United States.

In 1917, Big Bill Haywood of the IWW had a meeting here to decide on a defense strategy for himself and 165 other union members who were indicted under the Espionage Act in Chicago for impeding the war effort by encouraging people to avoid the draft. This attempt to shut down the IWW resulted in long, punitive prison sentences and fines of $2.5 million. But Big Bill jumped bail and escaped to the Soviet Union, where he eventually died, sadly disillusioned after Lenin's promises to organize worker-run factories never materialized.

In 1936, the American Labor Party (ALP) was founded at the Brevoort Hotel by union leaders Sidney Hillman and David Dubinsky, as well as Barney Vladek of the *Jewish Daily Forward*. Set up as a vehicle for socialists to vote for Franklin Delano Roosevelt for president without having to pull the lever for the Democratic Party, the ALP later also gave birth to the Liberal Party from members who were anti-communist.

The hotel finally closed in 1948; it was felt that even after renovation, it would still fail new fire safety codes. In 1955, the current Brevoort Apartments were built.

Remember that you are standing on land that once belonged to African slave Simon Congo, though the building is named for Hendrick Brevoort, a rich Dutchman who later owned eighty-six acres of land stretching north to Fourteenth Street. The Brevoort family name is on several buildings in the area. Simon Congo's name is on none.

❺   12 EAST EIGHTH STREET—Max Eastman lived here in a room on the second floor in long-time friend Eugen Bossevain's apartment. Bossevain married Edna St. Vincent Millay, and lived in the "narrowest house in the Village" (see Greenwich Village II Tour).

❻   WEINSTEIN HALL (5-11 University Place)—In the summer and fall of 1970, a series of dances were held at this NYU dormitory by the Gay Liberation Front and the Christopher Street Liberation Day Committee. They were eventually cancelled because, as an NYU Vice Chancellor said, "[impressionable freshman]...could swing both ways."

In September of that year, up to 100 people organized a sit-in in the sub-basement of this building for seven days. The students above them voted to have the dances, but NYU ultimately prevailed: New York City's Tactical Patrol Force (riot police) were sent in, and a crowd of four hundred people were kicked out of the building with twenty-nine getting arrested. Among the protester's demands were free tuition for all gay people and other oppressed minorities, and an end to the teaching of myths and lies about gay people. Though this action didn't immediately change NYU's policy, it was part of the massive post-Stonewall uprising of the gay and lesbian community, which got more and more visible every month.

Though not the same building, this was the site where the

Triangle Shirtwaist Factory moved its operations after the horrible 1911 fire (see Greenwich Village I Tour).

⑦ WASHINGTON SQUARE CHURCH (135 West Fourth Street)—Built in 1860, this church also has a progressive history. Paul Abels, the pastor from 1973 to 1984, was the first openly gay minister in a major Christian denomination in the U.S. He began conducting wedding ceremonies for gay couples, and finally left the church over the national Methodist conference, which voted to bar gays and lesbians from the clergy. He died of AIDS in 1992.

The Harvey Milk School—now at the Hedrick Martin Institute at 2 Astor Place—for gay and lesbian high school students, started here.

In the 1960s, Reverend Finley Schaef donated $40,000 to the Black Panthers, and during the Sunday service the Panthers spoke to the parishioners.

Vietnam War resisters came here for draft counseling, and Daniel Berrigan and Jane Fonda spoke here. During a service where draft resisters openly declared their resistance, police entered the church and dragged them away. During the Gulf War, the militant and inspiring high school group, Students Against War, held their meetings here. In the 1980s, Mobilization for Survival, one of New York City's leading anti-nuclear groups, had their offices here and most recently, in the mid-90s, the Committee in Support of the Zapatistas met here.

The women's movement had a very important event here in 1970, when abortion was still illegal in New York State. Before the Roe vs. Wade decision by the Supreme Court in 1973, New York women established their own test case, Abramowicz vs. Lefkowitz, which was being heard by the U.S. (Southern) District Court. However, Judge Edward Weinfield decided that women testify too "personally and emotionally," and he wouldn't allow those women who had had an abortion to testify in open court; they could only tes-

Washington Square Church—a site of activism to this day.
PHOTO BY PETER JOSEPH

tify through deposition. The outraged women's movement set up in the church to take live testimony with a large media presence, but an assistant district attorney interrupted the proceedings and everyone trooped down to the federal courthouse for a ruling by the judge.

Due to pressure from the women's movement, the judge relented and women such as Grace Paley and Susan Brownmiller gave testimony. Unfortunately, or fortunately, the case did not become a national precedent because while a decision was pending, the New York State Legislature overturned the anti-abortion laws and New York State got abortion rights three years before the 1973 Supreme Court decision. The great radical women's group Redstockings also had a speak-out at the church on abortion in 1969.

8 **MAX EASTMAN'S APARTMENT (118 Waverly Place)**—Max lived here twice, the first time with his activist-sister, Crystal Eastman, from 1909 to 1911. Max was one of the leading radicals and intellectuals in the Village, a lifelong Trotskyist, an editor of *The Masses* magazine and its successor, *The Liberator*. He was an enemy of Communists for most of his life, and he organized the Men's League for Woman Suffrage and spoke all over the state about a woman's right to vote. He married Ida Rauh (see Greenwich Village I Tour) in 1911 and, after they divorced in 1914, returned to this apartment where he paid $55 per month in rent.

The repression against the left during WWI resulted in *The Masses'* staff being brought up twice on charges of conspiring to obstruct the draft under the Espionage Act. Both trials resulted in hung juries, though the magazine was forced out of business after its mailing license was taken away. *The Liberator* was started by Max and Crystal Eastman in 1918, and for some reason was not attacked, though the Palmer Raids of 1920 led to four thousand arrests in thirty-three cities and one thousand deportations nationwide. Eastman wrote many books during his lifetime; he died in 1969 at the age of eighty-six.

9 THE SITE OF *THE MASSES* MAGAZINE OFFICE (91 Greenwich Avenue)—*The Masses* was the bohemian magazine of the Village in the 1910s, ending its run in a building previous to the one now on the site. *The Masses* was a noncommercial publication that represented artists, Freudians, Marxists, free-love advocates, and all-around rebels. Though its circulation never rose above fourteen thousand, it had worldwide influence and featured the likes of John Reed writing about the Paterson Silk Strike of 1913, poet Claude McKay, still-relevant one-panel cartoons, and the works of artists like John Sloan and Art Young.

Two trials by the government and the suspension of mailing privileges shut it down. Its successor, however, *The Liberator*, grew to a circulation of sixty thousand. It featured, for instance, the articles that became John Reed's *Ten Days That Shook the World*. In a major error made by editor Floyd Dell, *The Liberator* is now famous for rejecting early works of soon-to-be-famous poet Langston Hughes.

10 GOLDEN STAIR PRESS (23 Bank Street)—This small publishing company was founded by Langston Hughes, Carl Van Vechten, and Prentiss Taylor in 1931. It published Hughes's poetry as well as a booklet on The Scottsboro Boys case.

11 CONDOMANIA (351 Bleecker Street)—This store opened in 1991, during Gay Pride Week. Though certainly tourist oriented, Margaret Sanger would never have believed she would see the day that condom stores were opening all over the country. Condoms go back hundreds of years, originally made out of sheepskin and designed not for birth control, but for protection against venereal disease.

Condoms became widespread in the U.S. after WWI, because American troops were coming down with syphilis at such high rates. The armed forces gave out millions of condoms during the war and, ironically, distributed a previously government-censored article by Margaret Sanger on birth control, after conviently deleting her byline.. The development of vulcanized rubber in the late nineteenth century made condoms more effective and convenient. By the 1930s, the fifteen chief makers of condoms were producing 1.5 million per day.

Condoms have been a big part of the gay rights movement. ACT-UP organized condom distribution at high schools in the early 90s, through its group YELL (Youth Education Life Line).

⑫ ABBIE HOFFMAN'S LIBERTY HOUSE (343 and 345 Bleecker Street)—In 1966, Abbie Hoffman came to New York for the second time to establish Liberty House, a crafts cooperative, set up by the Student Non-Violent Coordinating Committee (SNCC) of Mississippi. It sold crafts made by African Americans in the South, and split the money between those who made the crafts (imagine that happening under capitalism!) and the local SNCC branch. Abbie met his second wife, Anita, here; she volunteered to help with the store while she was a graduate student at Yeshiva University. They married in Central Park, behind the Metropolitan Museum of Art, popularizing a tradition of park weddings that continues to this day.

⑬ FORMER POLICE PRECINCT (135 Charles Street)— This building went up in the mid-1890s, and still bears remnants from its days as the Ninth, and then Sixth, Precinct. However, its most important history involves a police raid on a gay bar called the Snake Pit, at 211 West Tenth Street. Over 160 men were rounded up and brought to this precinct in 1970, eight months after the Stonewall riots.

They were not told what they were charged with, and not allowed to make phone calls. They did sing and chant, in solidarity, *We Shall Overcome* and *Gay Power, Gay Power.*

One man, Diego Vinales, was so frightened over his arrest that he jumped out the second-floor window of the precinct, impaling himself on the iron fence outside. Firemen used a blowtorch to take apart the fence to transport him to St. Vincent's Hospital, the spikes still in his body. Initially in a coma, he was in the hospital for three months, where the NYC Police Department charged him with attempted escape.

The Gay Activists Alliance organized a march and vigil of five hundred people from the precinct to the hospital and finally to Sheridan Square. All charges were ultimately dropped against the men and the resulting publicity and protest caused the police department to transfer two hundred plainclothes officers from persecution of gay men to the Narcotics Division. Deputy Inspector Seymour Pine, of the "Public Morals Section," ordered both this raid and the Stonewall raid of 1969.

Across the street, 144 Charles Street, was the site of *The Catholic Worker* newspaper, the radical Catholic newspaper founded by Dorothy Day in 1933. It was here from 1935 to 1936, at which time it had a circulation of sixty-five thousand. (See the East Village II Tour.)

I used to take my tours to 681 Washington Street, the home of Judith's Room bookstore from 1989 to 1995, but unfortunately the last women's bookstore in NYC closed. It had great books, t-shirts, magazines and readings, but was in a poor location. Also, thanks to the women's movement of the 1960s, most bookstores now have a women's section. But the sections are usually not as good as in an independent bookstore. Through the years, I was always saddened when, upon talking about this bookstore, I was asked by a woman, "What's a women's bookstore?" Were the 1960s that long ago?

The East Village

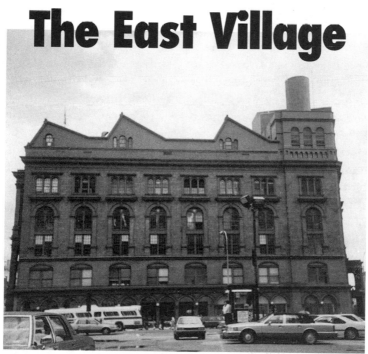

Here's a little-known fact: the East Village doesn't exist; it's actually the Lower East Side. The name came about this way: In 1956, the Third Avenue elevated train tracks were taken down, and in 1961 the expensive Stewart House went up on Tenth Street between Broadway and Fourth Avenue. The real estate industry saw they could sell and rent apartments more easily by calling the area east of Greenwich Village "the East Village."

It was marketed toward those frozen out of Greenwich Village, and its closeness to Wall Street was emphasized. However, the area has always served as a landing place for immigrants, and the battle continues; will the neighborhood turn into a Yuppie haven, or remain working-class? The riots at Tompkins Square Park in recent years, and the exodus of mom-and-pop stores due to rent increases, are signs of the battle.

Hundreds of years ago when an enemy's army was approaching, you knew you were in trouble. Nowadays, its the quiche places and Starbucks Coffee outlets that signal a war on the neighborhood. The Union Square area, known historically as a home for unions, has been transformed also, as large suburban stores have moved in, forcing out stores like Revolution Books, now at 9 West Nineteenth Street.

EAST VILLAGE I TOUR

❶ **ASTOR PLACE**—This open square is filled with history: 13 Astor Place was the United Auto Workers (UAW), District 65 building until the local went bankrupt and was replaced by apartments on the market for between $300,000 and $1,000,000. The building originally went up in 1890, and was used for events by progressive organizations when the union was there, including the Committee in Solidarity with the People of El Salvador, which held marvelous dances.

It now features a Starbucks Coffee on its main floor. The newsstand in front of Starbucks is the famous point where *The Village Voice* is first released, with long lines of people waiting every Tuesday night in what has become a Village ritual. *The Village Voice* offices are at 36 Cooper Square, and the workers used to be represented by District 65 of the UAW.

Astor Place is named for John Jacob Astor, one of New York City's most famous robber barons. When he died in 1848, he was the richest man in the world, and his family later owned many slum tenements on the Lower East Side.

Some clever artists altered the street signs a few years ago to make 'Astor Place' read 'Peltier Place,' after imprisoned American Indian Movement (AIM) activist Leonard Peltier. It was an irony wrapped in a word play, since the Astors first made their money by ripping off the Native Americans in the fur trade.

The giant black cube in the center of the square is a sculpture by Tony Rosenthal named "The Alamo." It went up in

East Village I

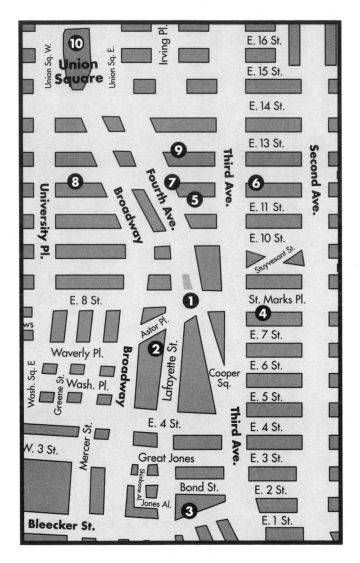

1967 and weighs three thousand pounds. It can be spun by two or more people but watch out for the skateboarders whizzing by.

The highlight of the square is the Cooper Union Building (41 Cooper Square, see photo on page 63), completed in 1854 and five years later housing the college of the same name. Founded by a benevolent capitalist—not a term I use often— Peter Cooper, the school was set up as free education for the working class, inspired by the Polytechnic Institute of France.

Peter Cooper knew there was no such thing as a self-made millionaire, hence he always gave back to the community by, for example, establishing the People's Institute, which gave progressive lectures to area residents. The building itself includes steel railroad track as girders, and was a major innovator in using steel in the development of the skyscraper, which we all take for granted today.

The circular shaft on the roof was made by Peter Cooper in anticipation of the invention of the elevator, not certain at the time if it would be circular or square. In 1975, the building was renovated with the exterior nineteenth-century walls retained for aesthetic reasons, but no longer structurally necessary.

The Great Hall in the basement has always been open to speakers of all political views, and some of the famous speakers over the years have included Frederick Douglass, Samuel Gompers, Peter Kropotkin, Norman Thomas, Susan B. Anthony, Abraham Lincoln, Amiri Baraka, Max Eastman, Margaret Sanger, Allen Ginsberg, Victoria Woodhull, and Daniel DeLeon. In 1883, there was a commemoration of Karl Marx's death, and four years later a protest against the impending Haymarket executions in Chicago. In the early 1990s, ACT-UP held their weekly, five hundred-person meetings here and, despite the large crowds when the late, great AIDS activist Bob Rafsky spoke, you could hear a pin drop.

One of the most famous actions in the Great Hall was the horsewhipping Emma Goldman gave her former mentor,

German anarchist Johann Most, after he denounced Alexander Berkman, Emma's lover, for his attempted assassination of Henry Clay Frick. Frick was the chief operating officer of the Carnegie Steel Works, whose vicious lock-out of the workers in Homestead, Pennsylvania resulted in the deaths of seven strikers after a twelve-hour battle with the union-busting Pinkerton detectives.

②   COLONNADE ROW (428-434 Lafayette Street)—This was a row of nine mansions, but only four of the original remain; Wannamaker's Department Store built its warehouse here, knocking down five of the buildings (the Wannamaker's name can still be glimpsed on the back of the building, south of the row). These 1833 buildings were where the richest people in the world lived, including John Jacob Astor, Cornelius Vanderbilt, and the Schermerhorn family. Lafayette Street used to stop at Great Jones Street, ensuring that the rich wouldn't see the people who produced their wealth. Like

Colonnade Row, formerly homes to the filthy rich. PHOTO BY BRUCE KAYTON

many expensive buildings in Manhattan, the stone was quarried by prisoners.

Across the street is the Public Theater (425 Lafayette Street), founded by the late Joseph Papp (see Central Park Tour). It was the first major public library and later the Hebrew Immigrant Aid Society (see the plaque on front of building and the fading acronym—HIAS—on the north wall). Though it appears to be one building, it is actually three buildings joined together, built in intervals between 1853 and 1881.

❸ THE WAR RESISTER'S LEAGUE BUILDING (339 Lafayette Street)—Known as the "Peace Pentagon," this building has been owned by the War Resister's League (WRL) since 1969. They moved here because their old office at 5 Beekman Place, near City Hall, was raided by the government, provoking the landlord to ask them to leave. Over seventy years old, the WRL organized the first peace demonstration against the Vietnam War, and ran an underground railroad to Canada at the same time. Its most famous members have included Albert Einstein, A.J. Muste, and David McReynolds. It rents space to other progressive groups, such as the Libertarian Book Club, Paper Tiger TV, and the Nicaragua Network.

The Nicaragua Network produces an excellent weekly update on topical issues in Central and South America, as well as the best listing of progressive political events in New York City. (They can be reached by telephone (212) 674-9499, and by web site at http://home. earthlink.net/~dbwilson/creed.html).

In the 1970s, this building housed the Free Space Alternate U, a radical school that featured, among other things, radical walking tours led by Bob Palmer and Scott Lewis.

Gazing across Houston Street you are looking at Soho (**South of Ho**uston Street). It has become a gentrified strip of cafes and art galleries, with late night clubs and large retail stores. The real estate industry's designation of the area in which you stand as Noho (**North of Ho**uston Street), has not exactly caught on.

❹   THE MODERN SCHOOL (6 St. Mark's Place)—This building housed the Francisco Ferrer Center of the anarchist Modern School, which featured Emma Goldman, Alexander Berkman, and Upton Sinclair on its board of directors. It later moved to Harlem, and then to Stelton, New Jersey, where it closed in 1953.

Inspired by the execution by firing squad of Francisco Ferrer by the Spanish government in 1909, it was set up to implement his teaching beliefs in a modern, progressive education. He hated government and organized religion, emphasizing equality, brotherhood, and cooperation. Over 120 schools were set up in Spain during his lifetime, before his execution on phony charges of inspiring a general strike in Spain.

In 1912, members of the Modern School took in the children of strikers during the Industrial Workers of the World's famous Lawrence, Massachusetts strike (see Webster Hall site below). In 1915, it became a Jewish bathhouse, then a gay bathhouse before being shut down in 1985 due to the AIDS crisis. The Modern School still holds reunions every year. Contact: Jon T. Scott at (518) 861-5544.

❺   WEBSTER HALL (119 East Eleventh Street)—Built in 1895, this now prominent night club has a long radical history. In 1912, then-Socialist Party member Margaret Sanger led 119 children of the Industrial Workers of the World-led Lawrence, Massachusetts "Bread and Roses" strikers in a march from the train station to have a meal here before being placed with supporters. Though their parents worked in the garment industry, the children wore tattered clothing as they voraciously ate their first decent meal in weeks.

The labor history of the building continued with the 1914 founding convention of the Amalgamated Clothing Workers of America (recently merged with the ILGWU to form UNITE!), led by Sidney Hillman as a move away from the more conservative United Garment Workers of America. The Amalgamated grew to over ninety thousand members, and

Sidney Hillman became an advisor to President Franklin Delano Roosevelt.

In the 1910s, *The Masses* held raucous costume balls here, some featuring nude revelers, as fundraisers for the always financially-pressed magazine. Other highlights at Webster Hall include various Emma Goldman speeches, and the meeting place of the New York Sacco-Vanzetti Defense Committee. In the 1950s, there were hootenannies, given by the group People's Artists, with Pete Seeger and Woody Guthrie occasionally dropping by.

6　SITE OF 208 EAST TWELFTH STREET (now an NYU dormitory)—This was the site of famous anarchist Carlo Tresca's newspaper, *Il Martello*, in the 1920s. Carlo fled to this country from Italy in 1904, where he constantly faced libel charges as he published revealing truths about promiscuous priests who preached abstention. He was involved with the Industrial Workers of the World, dated "Rebel Girl" Elizabeth Gurley Flynn, fought against Italian fascists here in America, and supported the Spanish Anarchists in the 1930s. His newspaper was shut down in 1923 because of a Margaret Sanger ad for birth control; he served six months in jail for this "crime."

An outspoken opponent of the Soviet Union, the mafia, and capitalism, he was gunned down at a nearby street corner in 1943 (see Chelsea–Ladies' Mile Tour).

7　WOMEN'S TRADE UNION LEAGUE (Corner of Fourth Avenue and Twelfth Street)—After its New York branch was established in 1903, the Women's Trade Union League (WTUL) regularly set up a stepladder on this corner for organizing speeches directed at the thousands of women leaving the factories at day's end. The WTUL was active at the Triangle Shirtwaist Factory strike of 1909, and held social picnics in Central Park as part of its mission to get more women into the union movement.

8 **WORKER'S LAB THEATER (42 East Twelfth Street)**—
This radical theater collective was established in 1929 to
reach the masses with political street theater. The core members of The Shock Troupe lived in the building, performing
full time at Union Square, workers' picnics, strike sites, and
in the subways. In the 1930s, they performed *World's Fair* in
opposition to Chicago's World Fair.

The tradition was continued in the early 1990s by the
Nicaragua Network's group Adelante!, which attacked politicians, the Gulf War, and racism at demonstrations, festivals
and on the subways. (While doing guerrilla theater in
Manhattan, I was amazed to learn how many public sidewalks are in reality privately owned.)

9 **CLARENDON HALL (112-114 East Thirteenth
Street)**—The Central Labor Union (CLU), founded in 1882,
held meetings here and at the Science Hall at 141 E. Eighth
Street. The first labor day parade in the United States was
planned here and held later in the year at Union Square (see
next site).

In 1886, the CLU invited four hundred delegates and 165
organizations here to fight an anti-labor mayoral campaign,
nominating progressive Henry George. He finished second
with sixty-eight thousand votes to Abram Hewitt, Peter
Cooper's political-hack brother-in-law, but beat out
Theodore Roosevelt, the Republican candidate, by eight
thousand votes.

In 1900, there was a meeting here to establish *The New
York Call*, the influential socialist newspaper which became
the unofficial organ of the Socialist Party (see City Hall Tour).
They featured the best coverage of the 1911 Triangle
Shirtwaist Fire.

10 **UNION SQUARE**—Named for the union of Broadway
and Fourth Avenue (not the large number of union headquar-

ters historically in the area), Union Square was completed in 1835 as one of several squares set up in Manhattan. Prior to this, it held squatters and a potter's field. In the 1840s, the rich bought up the area and lots around the square began selling for ten times their original $500 value.

In 1882, the first official labor day parade in the country took place here with nearly twenty-five thousand workers marching in demand of the eight-hour day, an end to both child labor and the contract system. The organizers, the Central Labor Union, urged workers to sever all ties to the Democratic and Republican Parties, and unite worldwide. Many in the crowd carried signs urging an end to rent, prompting a *New York Times* editorial declaring the signs, "grotesque in their disregard of the inevitable operation of the laws that regulate the relationship of men with each other."

This first labor day march is celebrated each year in September, in what has become a lackluster parade of out-of-touch officials; it's even been called off in some years due to low attendance.

The radical alternative, the May 1st International Worker's Day celebrations, started in 1886, when thirty thousand people marched at the behest of the American Federation of Labor, which was on the verge of collapse at the time. Three years later, the Socialist International or "Second International," made it a holiday for radicals, and by 1890 there were hundreds of demonstrations around the world, including thirty thousand people in Union Square. In the 1930s, between one and two hundred thousand marched until the mainstream unions pulled out in the 1940s.

In 1910, the ILGWU organized a rally of five thousand here, during the "Uprising of the Twenty Thousand." The following year, a funeral procession for the victims of the Triangle Shirtwaist Factory Fire marched from Washington Square to Union Square.

In 1927, on the eve of the execution of anarchists Nicola Sacco and Bartolomeo Vanzetti, machine guns were placed on the rooftops of the landmark S. Klein department store (since replaced by the luxury housing of Zeckendorf Towers in the mid-1980s) to intimidate the crowd that formed to protest their impending deaths. Carlo Tresca spoke at the rally.

One of the most famous demonstrations in Union Square was in 1930, when, during the depression, the Communist Party called for nation-wide demonstrations against unemployment. Over thirty-five thousand people turned up, despite Communist Party leader William Z. Foster having been urged by the government to call off the march. Three hundred police officers watched the crowd, and started beating demonstrators who wanted to march to City Hall. Over seven thousand would make the trip, but several Communist Party leaders were jailed for "inciting a riot." Fifty school children were picked up by truant officers, their parents being issued summonses. One month later, on International Worker's Day, thirty thousand marched in a peaceful rally, and the entire New York City Police Force of 18,300 was placed on alert.

In 1893, Emma Goldman was arrested for a speech to the unemployed, wherein she urged those without bread to take it. She spent a year in jail at Blackwell's Island (now Roosevelt Island), learning the nursing trade; she later earned two medical degrees in Europe.

Carlo Tresca spoke on International Worker's Day in 1914, denouncing those who killed thirty-three workers in the Ludlow, Colorado strike at the Rockefeller-owned Colorado Fuel and Iron Company. "Name the Murderer!" he thundered and the crowd called back "Rockefeller!"

On June 19, 1953, since the police refused to let organizers use Union Square, several thousand crowded Seventeenth Street adjoining the square to protest the impending execution of the Rosenbergs.

Union Square continued its radical tradition with lesbian rallies during Gay Pride Weekend, a march against the Israeli invasion of Lebanon in 1982, and a march in 1989 against the phony elections in El Savador. By this time, however, the old

Gandhi statue at Union Square. A New York rarity, in that it pays tribute to a non-violent individual. PHOTO BY PETER JOSEPH

political culture, with people spontaneously talking on soapboxes provoking discussion, was dead.

Union Square Park went through a $3.6 million renovation in the mid-1980s which made the park more sterile, making the area more upscale and anti communal as more chain stores moved in. However, the park does have a statue of Gandhi in its southwest corner (one of the few statues in New York City devoted to someone who hasn't murdered). I find it ironic, considering his hunger strikes, that he walks toward the Greenmarket fresh-food stalls that are set up several times a week.

The union-run Amalgamated Bank still adorns Broadway and the Sidney Hillman Health Center is still on Sixteenth Street between Broadway and Fifth Avenue. Paterson Silks, slated to move, on the corner of University Place and Fourteenth Street, is also a reminder of the famous Industrial Workers of the World 1913 Paterson, New Jersey strike (see Chelsea–Ladies' Mile Tour).

East Village II

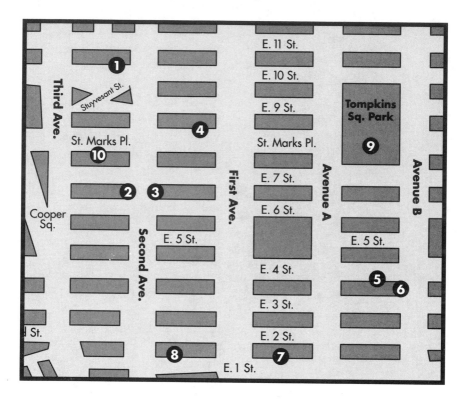

EAST VILLAGE II TOUR

❶ ST. MARK'S-IN-THE-BOWERY CHURCH (Corner of Second Avenue and Tenth Street)—Built in 1799, this is the oldest church site, but not the oldest church, in Manhattan. The adjoining Stuyvesant Street, laid out with a compass, is the only street in Manhattan to run exactly east-west. The street itself used to lead to Dutch Governor Peter Stuyvesant's estate, which was here in the seventeenth century, stretching approximately from Avenue A to Third Avenue, and from Third to Fourteenth Streets.

Stuyvesant was the last Dutch governor of New Amsterdam before the Dutch surrendered to the English in 1664, and renamed this small town "New York." He was dictatorial and racist; he owned forty slaves on his estate here. He died in 1672, and is buried in the vault on the north side of the church, visible from the cemetery. Seven generations of Stuyvesants are buried in the vaults in the church. The most notable person in the cemetery itself is former New York State Governor Daniel Tompkins, for whom Tompkins Square Park is named (see below).

The church itself has been progressive, supporting the Civil Rights movement, voter registration, prison reform, and opening the nation's first lesbian healthcare clinic. Here, Amy Lowell and Edna St. Vincent Millay staged poetry readings; Isadora Duncan danced, and Andy Warhol screened his early films. The Black Panthers and Young Lords held meetings here in the 1960s.

The St. Mark's Poetry Project dates back to 1966. Their New Year's Day Poetry Marathons are world famous and, over the years, have featured Allen Ginsberg, Penny Arcade, Jim Carroll, and Eileen Myles.

The small space in front of the church was the place to go in the 1960s to find out what was going on in the Village. During the occupation of Tompkins Square Park by the New York City Police Department, and its fifteen-month closing in 1991 and 1992, a march started here denouncing the police's verbal harassment of women, a constant occurrence.

2 **FILLMORE EAST (105 Second Avenue)**—The theater itself was knocked down in 1997, the old entrance being converted into the Emigrant Savings Bank. Bill Graham opened the Fillmore East in 1968, and it became one of the most famous rock 'n roll clubs of the 1960s. Elton John, Janis Joplin, Otis Redding, the Doors, the Grateful Dead, and Grace Slick all played here, with Joplin sometimes sleeping at Abbie Hoffman's apartment at 30 St. Mark's Place.

In 1969, the first staged performance of The Who's *Tommy* played here, and one night John Lennon joined with Frank Zappa and the Mothers of Invention. When Lennon lived in the Village at 105 Bank Street, before moving uptown to the Dakota in 1974, he would hang out with Abbie Hoffman and Jerry Rubin.

The Fillmore East closed in 1971, later to be a gay discotheque called The Saint. Previously, in the 1920s, it was a silent movie theater, then the Loew's Commodore movie theater, and a Yiddish theater in the 1930s. Many of the current theaters on Second Avenue, both theatrical and movie houses, were Yiddish theaters from the turn-of-the-century Jewish immigrant era.

3 **ISAAC HOPPER HOME (110 Second Avenue)**—This home honors the memory of Isaac T. Hopper, a major Quaker anti-slavery activist. He left the Quakers because they failed, early on, to be firmly anti-slavery. He came to New York City from Philadelphia to form the New York Association for Friends, a relief agency for slaves. He defended, in court, slaves being prosecuted under the Fugitive Slave Law. He eventually opened a bookstore on Pearl Street, selling some of his own writings against slavery.

Hopper was also active in reform for female prisoners, and he worked with the New York Prison Association in founding an early home for women coming out of prison.

After he died, a bequest was made in his memory in the 1850s; the house

Isaac Hopper, an early abolitionist and underground-railroad developer.
COURTESY OF PHOTOGRAPHS AND PRINTS DIVISION; SHOMBERG CENTER FOR RESEARCH IN BLACK CULTURE; THE NEW YORK PUBLIC LIBRARY; ASTOR, LENOX AND TILDEN FOUNDATIONS

was purchased, and it continues to this day as a thirty-day facility for women after their release from prison. It has eleven beds, and is run by the Women's Prison Association. They also run a larger apartment house on Avenue B adjoining Tompkins Square Park.

❹ 77 ST. MARK'S PLACE—This building was unfortunately redesigned in 1997. In 1917, while living at 1622 Vyse Street in the Bronx, Leon Trotsky worked on the bottom floor for *Novy Mir*, the Russian dissident newspaper.

He marveled at American technology while waiting for the Russian Revolution to start. Trotsky worked as a journalist, gave lectures in German and Russian, and was meeting with Eugene Debs, head of the U.S. Socialist Party, to start another newspaper, when things heated up in Russia. He left New York in March 1917 to make history.

There was a big farewell dinner in his honor before he left at the old Broadway Central Hotel on Broadway and Mercer Street, which subsequently collapsed and was replaced by an NYU dormitory.

❺ 232 EAST FOURTH STREET—This address has been replaced by 230 East Fourth Street due to the renovation of the building in the early 1990s. It was, however, a decaying walk-up where an unknown nineteen-year-old singer first lived when she came to New York City in 1978 with $37 in her pocket. The now multi-millionaire Madonna lived in this roach-infested fourth-floor walk-up and purportedly went 'dumpster-diving' in the local garbage containers for food when she wasn't begging restaurants for food (something many of the homeless and squatters in the area still do).

The renovation in the early 1990s replaced the windows and reopened the abandoned building so that it doesn't quite have the contrast with Madonna's current lifestyle that I was looking for. It's a reminder, however, of the pyramid-scheme nature of capitalism; Madonna "made it," but the rest of the neighborhood has not.

On the positive side, Madonna has given money to the anti-nuclear movement, the Central American Solidarity Movement, millions of dollars to the AIDS movement, and her videos have broken new ground in dealing with sexuality from a woman's perspective. However, when compared to people like Penny Arcade or Victoria Woodhull, Madonna looks very tame.

❻ BLACKOUT BOOKS (50 Avenue B)—This anarchist bookstore, with a great collection of books, opened several years ago. They've hosted interesting events featuring Earth

First!, the Atlantic Anarchist Circle, and Tom Gilroy, the from *Land and Freedom*. Instead of Barnes and Noble megastores on every other block in Manhattan, there should be more independent and radical bookstores like this one. The phone number is (212) 777-1967.

7 **JUSTUS SCHWALB'S SALOON (50 First Street)**—This radical saloon existed from the 1880s through the 1900s and was run by Justus Schwalb, one-time president of the Social Revolutionary Club. Saloons were very important as meeting places to radicals and immigrants at the turn of the century. This one featured a low ceiling, lots of smoke, and a working gun above the bar.

Schwalb was dragged to jail in 1870, after leading a demonstration at Tompkins Square Park and singing the Marseillaise. He persuaded his club to bring German anarchist Johann Most to America, who started *The Freiheit* newspaper and later served as Emma Goldman's mentor.

50 First Street—former site of Justus Schwalb's Saloon. PHOTO BY BRUCE KAYTON

Most was one of the few who actually fit the anarchist stereotype of bomb-making agitator. In a fit of anger in an argument with labor organizer Samuel Gompers, he smashed his beer mug so hard against a table that the glass dented the wall, dents that are said to still be visible in the first-floor room.

8 **CATHOLIC WORKER (36 East First Street)**—*The Catholic Worker* was founded in 1933 by Dorothy Day and Peter Maurin. It's a welcome sight, opposed to the Yuppie cafes and apartments in the area.

Dorothy Day worked for *The Masses* successor, *The Liberator*. She got arrested several times for fighting for the right to vote at the White House. Though religious, she strongly opposed the church hierarchy, with those at the top being rich and divorced from the life of the average worker.

Starting their famous one-cent newspaper on East Fifteenth Street, its circulation soared to 150,000 by 1936, since it talked about issues important to average people during the depression: the founding of the Congress of Industrial Organizations (CIO), strikes, communitarianism, and the evils of the wage system.

Farming communes were also organized, and houses of hospitality set up for food distribution and places to live. *The Catholic Worker* has been in this building since the 1960s, and its soup kitchen serves hundreds of men, with the women being served at the nearby Maryknoll House on East Third Street.

Dorothy Day died in 1980, but the radical Catholic perspective still continues in the one-cent *Catholic Worker* and pacifism and anti-draft work over the years. Day's autobiography, *The Long Loneliness*, remains a classic in the literature of religious-inspired radicalism.

9 **TOMPKINS SQUARE PARK**—Approaching the park along Avenue A, you'll notice the new Yuppie cafes and busi-

Tompkins Square Park. PHOTO BY PETER JOSEPH

nesses; you'll also see the double-decker buses of the mainstream tour businesses—always a bad sign.

One hundred-three Avenue A is the building where Julius and Ethel Rosenberg lived in 1940, one year after getting married. Ethel became active with the Communist Party front group "The East Side Conference to Defend America and Crush Hitler," which had an office at 137 Avenue B. Ethel helped organize a parade of seven thousand against Hitler and the Nazi Party, which drew one hundred thousand onlookers.

Tompkins Square Park was part of Stuyvesant's Meadow in the early 1800s. It was essentially swamp and marshland, until a descendant of Peter Stuyvesant sold it to New York City. The Government spent $93,000 to buy it, fill in the swamps, and plant trees. They named it for Daniel Tompkins, a vice-president of the United States under James Monroe, a governor of New York State (1807-1816), and a person who fought to abolish slavery, liberalize the criminal code, and relieve the poor of militia duty.

The rich got first crack at this beautiful park in the early nineteenth century, as the real estate industry built a row of homes on Tenth Street (299-319 East Tenth Street) that sold for $10,000 apiece. The row would have continued around the rest of the park, but for the 1837 depression which took the boom out of the market; one could see the row ends before reaching Avenue B.

Instead, Irish and German immigrants moved into the area, many of whom worked on the docks on the East River. Living conditions were abysmal; in the 1850s there were many demonstrations at Tompkins Square Park against unemployment and low wages. The State Legislature didn't like workers expressing their constitutional rights, so they paved over the parkland to make a military parade ground. However, the corrupt Tammany Hall (Democratic Party) head "Boss" Tweed used watered-down concrete and the new parade ground developed serious cracks over the next two years.

In January 1874, one of the most famous riots in the park occurred when the unemployed assembled in the park for a march to City Hall. Ten thousand workers and their families showed up, unaware that New York City had revoked the march permit the night before, and all hell broke loose. Police marched through the crowd on horseback, beating those who dared assemble, creating a bloodbath, prompting a strong *New York Times* editorial: "the forbearance and good humor of the police was admirable."

The following September, twenty-five hundred assembled to protest the police brutality.

In 1878, the parade grounds were turned into a park and ten thousand people attended its re-opening. One of those who fought to restore it as a park was Bernard Cohen, the grandfather of future NYC Parks Commissioner, and neighborhood destroyer, Robert Moses.

At the end of the nineteenth and early in the twentieth century, immigrants from Russia, Poland, and Eastern Europe arrived in this area, and many social service agencies followed. The Children's Aid Society opened at 127 Avenue B in 1887. Children entering through the basement were sprayed with Larkspur, a disinfectant.

The Tompkins Square Park Library was built in 1904 at 331 East Tenth Street, featuring books in seven languages to serve the immigrants. The Boys Club Headquarters at 287 East Tenth Street opened in 1901, and a Young Women's Settlement House opened in 1897, later changing its name to the Christadora House in 1914 and moving into 143 Avenue B in 1928.

The Christadora House featured free birth control, a library, swimming pool, and dental and health services. It was built to serve the community, and after being squatted in the 1960s by the Young Lords and the Black Panthers, it was sold in 1975 by the city in a sweetheart deal to a private investor who converted it into, what else, expensive apartments.

The Christadora House became a symbol of gentrification in the neighborhood. Many demonstrations in the 1980s and 1990s ended at this site for a round of window-breaking and protest.

Returning to the 1890s, the first municipal-run public baths in New York City were proposed for a corner of Tompkins Square Park but this was defeated by the community, which didn't want buildings taking up valuable park space.

In the 1950s and 1960s, a new wave of immigrants arrived—Puerto Ricans, Dominicans and Colombians—and public housing developments, named for Lillian Wald and Jacob Riis, went up east of the park. The area east of the park was eventually dubbed 'Loisaida.'

In the 1960s, the hippies arrived, as did the Psychodelicatessen on 293 East Tenth Street, the first head shop in the area. The bandshell, erected in 1966, featured Jimi Hendrix, Santana, the Fugs, and an early incarnation of the Grateful Dead. It's since been removed by the city.

Abbie Hoffman's first New York City demonstration was an anti-Vietnam War march in 1966, from Tompkins Square Park to Union Square. On Memorial Day of 1967, in a prelude to a history of fights with the police, local hippies and Puerto Ricans were stopped from playing conga drums as thirty-eight people were arrested after they linked arms and started resisting police violence. The judge ultimately threw out all charges, saying "this court will not deny equal protection to the unwashed, unshod, unkempt and uninhibited." Ah, the 1960s!

In the 80s, the real estate industry tried to force out the poor by setting buildings on fire or abandoning them altogether. Rents increased from one to four hundred percent, giving birth to a very mixed neighborhood: squatters, anarchists, yuppies, and artists. The area had appealed to artists looking for low-rent options in Manhattan, like Greenwich Village many years before, but in the 80s, the prices rose.

A major police riot occurred in August 1988; over four hundred police officers, many covering their name tags with tape, beat up protesters who were protecting the rights of the homeless to live in the park. One hundred-forty-seven complaints were filed with the Civilian Complaint Review Board, and officially forty-four people were injured.

The overzealous police made the mistake of beating up local yuppies, reporters, and business owners. Local video artist Clayton Patterson taped the riot, generating much publicity. Even Police Commissioner Benjamin Ward admitted, "I don't think there's any excuse for what happened." The mainstream media handled the affair as an aberration from typical police behavior, but those of us active in the fight to protect the park knew this was not the case.

The police occupation of the area lasted five full days, and

Tompkins Square Park, 1989. Police protecting the rights of landlords.
PHOTO BY CHRIS FLASH OF *THE SHADOW*

the fights continue against homeless encampments in the park.

1991 brought the famous Memorial Day Riot during a "Housing is a Human Right" concert. This battle between police and local residents served as a pretext for Mayor Dinkins to shut the park for "renovation" from June 1991 to August 1992. Police officers lined the sidewalks adjacent to the park by the hundreds, keeping people away from the large fence, alternately harassing women as they walked by.

At a time when the city was laying off thousands of workers and cutting social services, over $12 million was spent to maintain a large police presence, and to renovate the park to keep out the squatters and homeless. It was a cowardly move, part of the attack against the homeless all over the city, related to gentrification and a citywide "clean up" before the 1992 Democratic Convention came to town.

Hundreds tried to link arms around the park; there were protests all over the neighborhood. Acts of civil disobedience were committed, but the police enforced a rule that an activist's second arrest would lead to jail time, as opposed to getting a ticket for a future court appearance. The tactic was effective in stifling dissent.

The city also vindictively knocked down, in August 1991, the famous bandshell on the Seventh Street side of the park, a few days before a "Save the Bandshell" concert was slated. Now, a temporary bandshell is erected each time an event is organized, and performers must use the city-owned sound system.

I was very active in the attempt to fight the closing of the park, and witnessed much police brutality and dirty tactics by the city. Though there was tremendous police repression, there was also much divisiveness among local activists; the initial meetings saw hundreds of people, but there was an inability to keep them inspired.

Father Kuehn, formerly at St. Brigid's Church at 119 Avenue B, was a strong supporter; he presided over memorial services for homeless activist Terry Taylor in January 1994. Newly-elected Mayor Rudolph Guiliani had police arrest

Concert against police violence in Tompkins Square Park in the spring of '94.
PHOTO BY CHRIS FLASH OF *THE SHADOW*

The memorial service for homeless activist Terry Taylor, 1994. PHOTO BY CHRIS FLASH OF *THE SHADOW*

those carrying a mock coffin in Terry's memory around the corner from the church. St. Brigid's Church held many meetings on its front steps during the closing of the park for two straight summers in 1991 and 1992.

Other important sites around the park are Nino's Pizza at 131 Avenue A, which looked like a police precinct during the closing of the park. Its profits shot up, as those of other businesses around the park went down.

The Sarah Powell Huntington House at 347 East Tenth Street is run by the Women's Prison Association as permanent housing for women just released from prison.

One hundred fifty-one Avenue B, between Ninth and Tenth Streets, was the residence of jazz great Charlie Parker from 1950 to 1954; the block was subsequently named Charles Parker Place.

⑩   30 ST. MARK'S PLACE—St. Mark's Place served as the meeting place and hangout for all of those fleeing conventional society and flocking to the counter-culture.

This particular apartment building housed Abbie and Anita Hoffman in 1967, which Abbie described as a "$101 per month front row seat to the cultural revolution." Here, in December 1967, Paul Krassner and the Hoffmans came up with the idea of the "Yippies," or Youth International Party, as a vehicle to combat the "Convention of Death": The 1968 Democratic Convention in Chicago.

Abbie was arrested six times for loitering on his own block. He organized, among other things in his long career as an activist, a be-in in Central Park, the levitation of the Pentagon, and helped end the Vietnam War.

One of his famous actions was dumping hundreds of dollar bills on the floor of the New York Stock Exchange to watch the Wall-Streeters scramble and fight for the money, forcing them to act out a condensed version of what their lives were about.

His books live on, inspiring many of us who have continued organizing in the years after his death. We recall his sense of humor, zest for life, and belief in fighting for what is right. Many people flocked to this block to pay tribute to him after he died in 1989.

Across the street at 33 St. Mark's Place was a clothing store called Manic Panic, a trendy East Village shop. To get an idea of the gentrification of the area, their rent went from $250 per month in 1977 to $3,000 per month in 1988, and they were forced to move to a basement on Seventh Street. Many other local businesses haven't been so lucky, and eventually were forced to close due to high rents.

Chelsea

The Chelsea area's official borders are Sixth to Tenth Avenues and Fourteenth to Thirty-fourth Streets, but we are going to be creative and end this tour in upper Greenwich Village. Chelsea was named after England's Chelsea Royal Hospital by Thomas Clark, whose estate in 1750 stretched from Eighth Avenue to the Hudson River and Fourteenth to Twenty-fourth Streets. Over the years, Chelsea included Tin Pan Alley—where many popular songwriters got their start—elegant department stores, and a large amount of New York City nightlife.

The International Ladies Garment Workers Union middle-income housing units—over twenty-eight hundred apartments—went up in 1962, and currently occupy Twenty-third to Twenty-ninth Streets between Eighth and Ninth Avenues.

Union Organizer A. Philip Randolph (see Harlem tour) spent some of his later years here. Chelsea currently features several social service agencies, a large gay and Latino population, and the first openly HIV-Positive City Council member, political activist and ACT-UP member, Tom Duane.

CHELSEA—LADIES' MILE TOUR

❶ THE CHELSEA HOTEL (222 West Twenty-third Street)—This is Chelsea's most famous landmark (see photo on page 91), built in 1883 as co-operative apartments, becoming a hotel in 1905. Many of the famous robber barons stayed here, like J.P. Morgan and Andrew Carnegie. Also, the theater district was nearby in the late nineteenth century, so those involved in theater came here.

Later on, many famous writers stayed here, like Arthur Miller, Trotskyist James Farrell, Mark Twain, and O'Henry. In the 1960s, many figures in rock stayed here—the Allman Brothers, the Jefferson Airplane, and Pink Floyd, for instance. In the 1980s, noted punk rocker Sid Vicious of the Sex Pistols stabbed his girlfriend to death here; he died of a drug overdose before his trial started.

The radical history begins with Valerie Solanas, the founder of the Society for Cutting Up Men (SCUM), who was staying here at the time she shot artist Andy Warhol in June 1968. She had written the SCUM Manifesto the year before, which is now a feminist classic, even though much of it is tongue-in-cheek (Cost: $2 to men, $1 to women). She was angry at Warhol for not filming her script and for exploiting women in his films.

Ms. Solanas served three years in jail and was institutionalized, dying in 1988. Warhol said he didn't take life seriously until after this attempt on his life. He died in 1987, at New York Hospital, in what was perhaps a botched operation.

Chelsea-Ladies' Mile Tour

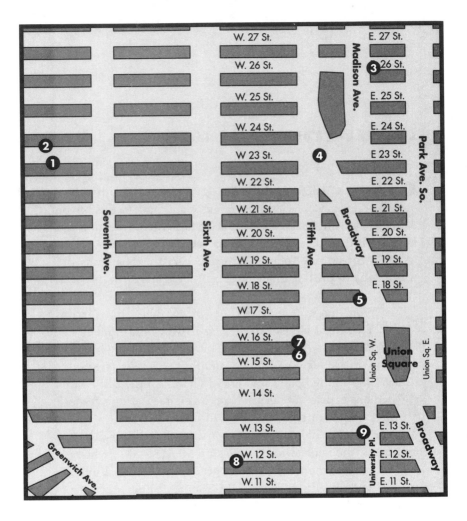

② **COMMUNIST PARTY HEADQUARTERS (235 West Twenty-third Street)**—Since the mid-1970s, this has been the national and local headquarters of the Communist Party, with the Unity Bookstore on the first floor. Four-time presidential candidate Gus Hall has been General Secretary since 1957, and a party member since 1927. When *Daily Worker* members protested his control and the need for new membership in the early 1990s, they were locked out of their offices and fired.

An offshoot of the Communist Party, The Committee of Correspondence formed and included long-time Communist Party member Angela Davis. The split is reminiscent of the infighting upon the inception of the Communist Party in America, in the late 1910s and early 1920s, when the Socialist Party endured splits and government raids. It was never the power that it had been in the 1910s, with one thousand municipal officers, including mayors in twenty-two cities, and over nine hundred thousand votes for president for Eugene Debs in 1920 while he served a prison term for speaking out against WWI.

In 1927, the national headquarters of the Communist Party moved from Chicago to New York City, and in 1929, took the name Communist Party.

As one heads east on Twenty-third Street toward Madison Square Park, look down Sixth Avenue for some remnants of the Ladies' Mile department stores from the turn of the century.

The Ladies' Mile was a fashionable shopping district of the late nineteenth century, though most of the women I concentrate on in this era did not see themselves as shopping machines. The former Ehrich Brother's Store went up in 1889 (699-709 Sixth Avenue), and included sweatshops upstairs; the Hugh O'Neill building (655 Sixth Avenue, with the name still visible at the top exterior) went up in 1887, and the former Adams and Company Dry Goods Store (675 Sixth Avenue, currently a Barnes and Noble superstore with the initials "ADG" still visible outside) went up in 1900.

These stores were the beginning of the modern department store era, and represent a tremendous accumulation of capital and products for the benefit of a few people, as more and more goods were sold by fewer and fewer corporations.

Another beautiful remnant of this era is the old Stern's Dry Goods Store at 32-46 West Twenty-third Street. There are actually two buildings there, meant to look like one; numbers 32-36 went up in 1878 and numbers 38-46 in 1892.

❸   THE NEW YORK LIFE INSURANCE COMPANY BUILDING (51 Madison Avenue, across from Madison Square Park)—This headquarters went up in 1928, but more importantly sits on the site of the first two Madison Square Gardens.

The first Madison Square Garden was officially opened in 1879, on the remains of Commodore Cornelius Vanderbilt's New York and Harlem Railroad's freight shed, before the railroad moved to the present site at Grand Central Station. Master showman P.T. Barnum put on shows here, after paying $35,000 to remodel the freight yards and erect twenty-eight-foot walls.

The second Madison Square Garden was completed in 1890 for the price of $3 million, replacing the earlier incarnation with a magnificent Stanford White design. Mr. White was one of the most famous architects, and womanizers, in New York City history. In 1906, he was killed on the roof of his creation by a jealous and deranged Pittsburgh capitalist named Harry K. Thaw.

The second Garden had a giant restaurant, a concert hall, eighty-foot-high ceilings, and an auditorium that held eight thousand people. It epitomized the Gay 90s era; the average woman attending the annual horse show wore $13,000 worth of jewelry. However, it cost $20,000 per month to maintain, and it finally went bankrupt in 1913, with the New York Life Insurance Company holding the $2.3 million mortgage. They subsequently decided to knock it down and erect its current headquarters building.

Before going bankrupt, there were two major events held at the second Madison Square Garden. In 1913, thirteen thousand silkworkers went on strike in Paterson, New Jersey, led by the Socialist Party and the Industrial Workers of the World (IWW).

Margaret Sanger organized children's marches to help publicize the strike and the fact that sympathetic New Yorkers were watching the children while the parents struck. There were many arrests in Paterson, and one worker was killed by detectives hired to harass the workers.

Big Bill Haywood, one of the leaders of the IWW, complained at Mabel Dodge's Salon (see Greenwich Village I Tour) on Fifth Avenue about the lack of sympathy for the strikers in the mainstream press (sound familiar?).

They walked to Haywood's mistress's house and Mabel Dodge came up with the idea of having the Greenwich Village bohemians produce a play about the strike at Madison Square Garden—it became *The Paterson Pageant*. John Reed was designated to direct the play, John Sloane to paint giant murals, and the strikers and strike leaders were to play themselves. The cost of the production kept rising and cuts had to be made in the number of scenes, but on June 7, 1913, fifteen hundred strikers made their way to the local train station to board a special thirteen-car train to Manhattan.

Carlo Tresca (see below) led a contingent of eight hundred marchers from the train to the Garden, and at 7:30 PM, the large neon letters of the IWW beamed from the rooftop of the Garden. Fifteen thousand workers attended the pageant, and Carlo Tresca and Big Bill Haywood made the same speeches they had made during the strike. However, ticket prices had to be drastically reduced, so the production lost a lot of money, negating an anticipated contribution to the strike fund.

Thousands of strikers who couldn't get on the special train complained, and there were accusations of theft. However, everyone from Margaret Sanger to John Reed made loans, not expecting to get paid back, and everyone realized it was an honest financial disaster.

The strike collapsed in July 1913, as did the alliance between the Socialist Party and the IWW, and only one good thing came out of the loss. Margaret Sanger got so disgusted with the Socialist Party and the labor movement, that she decided to devote herself to the birth-control movement (see below).

The other important event at the second Garden was in 1920; the first International Convention of the Negro Peoples of the World, organized by Black Nationalist Marcus Garvey. The convention of people from all over the world lasted for thirty days, but opening night saw an overflow crowd of almost twenty-five thousand people.

Its Declaration of Rights listed twelve complaints and fifty-four demands, in an attempt to unite Blacks from all over the world. For its remaining sessions, after the first night, the convention moved to Liberty Hall on West 138th Street (since demolished).

Such enthusiasm represented the height of Marcus Garvey's influence, and the Universal Negro Improvement Association, which he founded.

4 **THE FLATIRON BUILDING (175 Fifth Avenue)**— Erected in 1902, this architectural jewel housed the Socialist Labor Party's headquarters in the 1910s. The Socialist Labor Party is the oldest radical political party still in operation in the United States, with one member left in New York City. Almost all radical political parties originally spring from this group. Formed in 1876 in Philadelphia by German immigrants, it was originally called the Workingman's Party.

It gained fame under the leadership, or dictatorship, of Daniel DeLeon, who edited the newspaper for almost twenty-five years (1892-1914). DeLeon was dogmatic and authoritarian, and though his political program made sense, he had a hard time finding loyal adherents. Eventually, a Socialist Labor Party member named Morris Hillquit left with thousands of others to found the Socialist Party. Others got so dis-

The famous Flatiron Building. PHOTO BY MYRNA KAYTON

gusted with Mr. DeLeon that they started the *Jewish Daily Forward* in opposition to his party newspaper.

At approximately where East Twenty-fifth Street meets Madison Square Park is where Diane Keaton in *Reds*, playing John Reed's future wife Louise Bryant, disembarks from a horse-drawn carriage upon arriving in New York City from Oregon on her way to Reed's Greenwich Village apartment.

Heading down Broadway to Seventeenth Street, you will see more examples of the Ladies' Mile department stores, some of which now house suburban-style stores, thanks to changes in zoning laws, which further make Manhattan resemble a gigantic shopping mall.

⑤ EMMA GOLDMAN AND THE CORNER OF BROADWAY AND SEVENTEENTH STREET—This was the location of Emma Goldman's massage parlor in 1905, though an exact address is difficult to determine. She described her office as being on the top floor, having much air and sunlight and a view of the East River. With so many tall office buildings going up in subsequent years, such a river view is long gone.

Emma Goldman spent many years working in sweatshops of the Lower East Side, but she also had some successful businesses that enabled her to use more time for revolutionary organizing. In the 1890s, she started a dressmaking cooperative that failed in New Haven, Connecticut, and then set up a photography studio in Worcester, Massachusetts with Alexander Berkman, her nearly lifelong comrade, that also went under.

Her success started with an ice-cream parlor in Massachusetts, which she was forced to close in order to work on the Homestead, Pennsylvania strike of 1892. She later worked as a nurse, and then went into body massages in 1903.

Emma's body massages required much time, so her manicurist suggested she do only facial and scalp massages, which wouldn't require so many hours. Emma thought it dubious that women would flock to the notorious "Red Emma" for massages, but the manicurist recommended clients and her friend Bolton Hall lent her $300 to get started.

She took an office on one of these street corners, and soon had women clients from all types of professions, whom she served as a masseuse and quasi-therapist. Most of these professional women, according to Emma, were financially independent, but emotionally dependent on men and marriage.

Her clients liked her, and Emma began to get so successful that she thought of hiring a secretary, but she was obviously repulsed by a worker-management relationship. The dilemma was solved when the landlord, after discovering she was the famous "Red Emma," failed to renew the lease. She closed up shop and started the magazine *Mother Earth.*

❻ CARLO TRESCA AND THE CORNER OF FIFTH AVENUE AND FIFTEENTH STREET (Northwest Corner)— This was where anarchist Carlo Tresca was gunned down by a Mafia hitman on January 11, 1943. Carlo was involved in many fights during his lifetime, including the Industrial Workers of the World's Bread and Roses Strike of 1912, the fight to prevent the execution of fellow anarchists Sacco and Vanzetti, the fight against both fascists and Stalinists in Spain in the 1930s, and against an established newspaper publisher in America, Generosa Pope, who tried to cover up his previous support of Benito Mussolini.

On the night of January 11, 1943, Carlo was at the office of his newspaper, *Il Martello* (The Hammer), at 96 Fifth Avenue (the southwest corner, though the building isn't there anymore) leaving at 9:30 PM with his friend Giuseppe Calabi. They walked to the northwest corner, when future Mafia boss Carmine Galente emerged from the shadows and shot Carlo.

The police arrived and Carlo was pronounced dead on arrival at St. Vincent's Hospital. Thousands of supporters joined his funeral procession, with fifteen cars filled with flowers, and ten cars filled with reporters. Among those speaking at the funeral at Fresh Pond Cemetery in Queens were David Dubinsky, Norman Thomas, and Max Eastman.

Tresca's political work inspired much ire, so theories abound concerning who paid Galente to kill him. The official investigation didn't go far; investigators feared connection to prominent people. Galante served a year in jail, confessed to the crime, but claimed later that he didn't do it.

In 1979, Galente was gunned down at an Italian restaurant in Little Italy. In what became a famous front-page newspaper photograph, he lay dead with a cigar in his mouth.

❼ MARGARET SANGER'S BIRTH CONTROL CLINIC (104 Fifth Avenue, 20th Floor)—This 1911 building housed the first doctor-directed birth control clinic in the United States in the late 1910s. Originally set up to answer letters to the editor of her magazine *The Birth Control Review*, she eventually hired a doctor and catered to women desperate for birth control.

The first birth control clinic in the U.S. was set up by Margaret Sanger in Brownsville, Brooklyn in 1916, but it was illegal for a doctor to prescribe birth control, and hence no doctors would get involved. But a loophole in the law during her 1918 trial allowed her to hire a doctor, Dr. Hannah Stone, who created a contraceptive jelly, and kept medical records on thousands of women regarding abortions, miscarriages, and sexual behavior.

Publicity from Ms. Sanger's court battles and fights with the censors enabled her to outgrow this office, and move to a building at 46 West Fifteenth Street. She fought for most of her long life for the increased dissemination of birth control, but before becoming America's birth control pioneer, she was active in the Socialist Party, major strikes in the northeast, and is believed to have first learned about birth control from Emma Goldman, who used to smuggle early diaphragms (called pessaries) to the U.S. from Europe in the 1890s.

Ms. Sanger married the head of 3-In-1 Oil, Noah Slee, and in the 1920s pessaries were smuggled to the U.S. in 3-In-One oil drums via Europe and Canada. Slee eventually bought his wife a new building at 17 West Sixteenth Street. Planned Parenthood, the current well-known birth control clinic, was formed due to Ms. Sanger's work; her grandson, Alexander Sanger, now heads the local New York City office. The corner of Mott and Bleecker Streets, where the New York City office is located, was recently designated Margaret Sanger Square.

⑧ THE NEW SCHOOL FOR SOCIAL RESEARCH (66 West Twelfth Street)—The New School was founded in 1918 by dissident professors from Columbia University, furious over the firings of two professors for counseling their students to resist the World War I draft and oppose U.S. entry into the war. This was a time of repression against the left, with little or no free speech rights for those opposing the war.

For instance, during this era the Socialist Party and the Industrial Workers of the World were nearly shut down by the government, and radical publications like *Appeal to Reason* (the number-one circulating magazine in the country) and *The Masses* (see Greenwich Village III Tour) lost their mailing "privileges," and were forced out of business.

Eugene Debs, the head of the Socialist Party, was jailed for making a speech against the war in Ohio, and fellow Socialist Party member Rose Pastor Stokes faced ten years in jail for an anti-war letter to the editor of a Kansas newspaper.

Professors Charles Beard and James Harvey Robinson were so incensed over Columbia University President Nicholas Murray Butler's firing of two professors, that they resigned and began planning the New School with several associate editors of *The New Republic*, which at that time was politically to the left of *The Nation*.

Classes began at six brownstone mansions on West Twenty-third Street, thanks to the commitment of Dorothy Straight (an heir to the Whitney fortune) of $10,000 per year for ten years. Major principles of the school included faculty control, no endowment, and no real estate ownership. These principles soon gave way, and this building officially opened in 1931.

In the late 1920s, Mexican muralist Jose Orozco painted five murals in the building, including a controversial one of Lenin, Stalin and Gandhi, still preserved in Room 712. In the 1950s, during the era of McCarthyism, the board of trustees ordered a curtain placed over Lenin and Stalin after it was found that it couldn't be erased without tearing down the walls it was painted on. The Mexican government has since paid to preserve it, and it is a true sight to see along three of the walls of the classroom.

Other highlights of the New School include W.E.B. DuBois teaching the first college-level Black Studies class in the country. In 1933, the University in Exile Program welcomed Jewish and/or Socialist professors and researchers fleeing from Nazi Germany; many ended up doing important research on fascism.

The school has since become more of an establishment institution, but it offers many great classes, especially in its thriving Adult Education Program, where I happened to teach a class called "Jewish History of New York City."

⑨   116 UNIVERSITY PLACE (at Thirteenth Street)—This building was rented out by the Socialist Workers Party (SWP) from the late 1930s to the mid-1960s. Previously, the Socialist Party (SP) rented two floors in the building. The Industrial Workers of the World had an office here as well on the second floor.

The SWP was supportive of Malcolm X, and they still publish and have the rights to many of his speeches. They sponsored several forums with Malcolm X over the years, including one here in 1964 about eight months before he was assassinated. He was a surprise guest who had returned from his second trip to Africa just a few days before. He answered false charges made against him that he inspired a gang called the "Blood Brothers," which was killing white people. Malcolm talked about the brave fight of the brothers in Algeria who were attacking the French colonizers, police brutality in New York City (some issues never change), Cuba, and China.

At this time, Malcolm X left the Nation of Islam, organized the Organization of Afro-American Unity, and was preparing to work with Martin Luther King, Jr., which was the FBI's biggest nightmare. (See the Harlem Tour for more sites from Malcolm X's life.)

Wall Street

The Wall Street area is a classic place for a Radical Walking Tour. Over the years it has been the target of many demonstrations and it probably has had the highest percent of nineteeth- and twentieth-century robber barons working within its boundaries than anywhere else in the country. Of course, originally the Wall Street area was the entirety of New York City, then known as New Amsterdam, during the initial Dutch occupation in the 1610s.

Everyone lived and worked below Wall Street in the early seventeenth century, which then sported the famous wall for which it is named. There were eighteen languages spoken in the colony.

The Dutch West India Company, which owned the colony—corporate ownership being less concealed in those days—would accept any European willing to work the land in what was then a very brutal place in which to survive. The Dutch needed soldiers to kill Native Americans and labor to develop a strong balance of trade with Europe and the Caribbean. Eventually, enslaved Africans—three hundred of them by the time the Dutch left in 1664—were used for the essential labor.

In the way Wall Street continues to be a center for labor exploitation, many of its streets follow the contours first laid down by the Dutch invaders in the seventeenth century. The English peacefully threw the Dutch Government out in 1664, and renamed the area "New York," after the Duke of York.

The Wall Street area features many American Revolutionary War sites, which attract large crowds, reminding one of a historical change; in the 1770s, and 1780s, it was okay to be revolutionary, but today we're all supposed to go home, watch TV, and buy as many products as we can charge on our credit cards.

WALL STREET AREA TOUR

❶ **BOWLING GREEN PARK (across the street from the American Museum of the American Indian—1 Bowling Green)**—This was the first official park in New York City (1733), and the British used to tax the American colonists a nominal one peppercorn per year for using it.

The green was used for lawn bowling, and the fence goes back to 1771. It is believed that on this site Governor Peter Minuet "bought" Manhattan from the Canarsie Native Americans of Brooklyn, who were passing through at the time. Allegedly, the island was bought for $24 worth of trinkets, but in point of fact, the Native Americans had no concept of private ownership and thought they were receiving a gift for a temporary European stay.

The museum itself is located in what was the Alexander Hamilton U.S. Custom House, built in 1907, also the site of the former Fort Amsterdam, which was built by slaves in 1628 as a military defense of the Dutch colony. It sat on the water—Battery Park is largely landfill—and was the starting point for the massacre of Native Americans by the Dutch.

When the Iroquois tribe obtained muskets from the Dutch and used them to decimate the Algonquin tribe, Governor Kieft of New Amsterdam saw an opportunity to get rid of the Algonquin for good. He sent out two brigades of soldiers, and they massacred a total of one hundred twenty Native Americans, with the soldiers carrying their severed heads back to Fort Amsterdam as souvenirs.

The massacres established a state of war between the Europeans and Native Americans, causing many Dutch to

Wall St. - Battery Park Tour

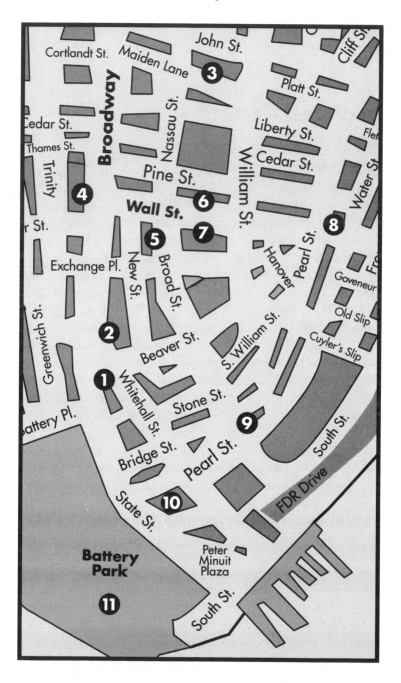

leave the colony and return to Holland. Others retreated to within Fort Amsterdam's walls. This led to a scarcity of food, and infuriated the Dutch West India Company, which had to send an additional one hundred fifty soldiers to New Amsterdam. Within a day, they slaughtered seven hundred Algonquin, then another five hundred Native Americans, in what is now Westchester County of New York.

Eventually, a temporary peace treaty was signed, but Governor Kieft was recalled to Holland to face charges of incompetence. On the return trip to the colonies he would, justifiably, drown, and be replaced by another dictator, Peter Stuyvesant (see East Village II Tour).

Across the street from the museum is 2 Broadway, a building that sold for $21 million in 1995, and is currently ninety percent empty. There was a building boom in the 1980s with a subsequent glut, resulting in many largely vacant skyscrapers. Many were erected with massive public subsidies and tax breaks, and when there was no demand for them, some landlords asked for subsidies from the government to tear them down.

②　26 BROADWAY (formerly the Standard Oil Company's Headquarters)—This building went up in the 1920s, replacing three smaller buildings on the site and serving as an imperial symbol of the Rockefeller oil empire. A perpetual oil flame burned at the top of the black cast-iron oil burner. The lobby had a statue of John D. Rockefeller and was emblazoned with the Standard Oil logo (SO).

Rockefeller was one of the most hated men of the late nineteenth century for his monopolizing of oil profits, which forced smaller companies out of business. He also used spies on the railroads to learn what other companies were shipping. In 1911, the Standard Oil Trust was broken up into individual state companies, though stock prices went through the roof, and Rockefeller and his son, along with fellow executives, made a killing.

The radical history starts in 1914, with the notorious Ludlow Massacre, the murder of thirty-three men, women and children during a vicious strike in Ludlow, Colorado against the Rockefeller-owned Colorado Fuel and Iron Company. Nine thousand miners went on strike against inhumane conditions, including company housing, consisting of two-room shacks at exorbitant rates, and payment in company scrip (money that could only be redeemed at the Rockefeller-owned general store).

They were fighting for the right to join the United Mine Workers. After the vicious eviction of the strikers from the company-owned housing into tents, a fight broke out between the mine guards and the strikers. The miners quickly ran out of ammunition, prompting the mine guards to charge through the tent colony and set it on fire. Eleven children and two women burned to death or suffocated from the smoke on the night of the massacre. Altogether, thirty-three strikers were killed during the seven-month strike.

President Woodrow Wilson eventually sent in the U.S. Army and the strikers were defeated.

In protest of the slaughter, Upton Sinclair, author of *The Jungle*, and many other great progressive books, organized a picket-line in front of 26 Broadway with mourners wearing black crepe paper. Marie Ganz, a Yiddish political activist from the Lower East Side (see Lower East Side I Tour), went up to Rockefeller's office and promised to kill him if another worker at one of his mines was killed. She was promptly arrested. There were protests against the Rockefeller empire at his estate in Tarrytown, New York, and at Standard Oil headquarters in Chicago and San Francisco. Though Upton Sinclair was a socialist, the Socialist Party criticized the action since it focused on an individual, and not against the capitalist system as a whole.

❸   MAIDEN LANE BETWEEN WILLIAM AND NASSAU STREETS—You are standing across from the back of the Federal

Reserve Bank of New York, erected in 1922 and currently holding $140 billion in gold, representing foreign holdings.

The Federal Reserve Bank first met in 1914; it has more
effect on the life of the country's workers than any elected
official/corporate puppet. It represents the central bank of the
United States in order to prevent what happened in the nineteenth century, when robber barons, like J.P. Morgan, served
as the central bank.

Maiden Lane was named by the Dutch in the seventeenth
century because it ran along a stream where the women (maid-
ens) would do laundry. Dutch New Amsterdam actually had
many bars and laundries, much like New York City today.

Maiden Lane was also the site of the first organzed slave
revolt in New York. On April 7, 1712, over twenty African
slaves set fire to the home of Peter Vantilborough—a slave-
owner. Nine members of the Vantilborough household and
neighboring estates were killed. The British caught, then sum-
marily tried, then killed thirty-nine Africans, either by torture
over fire or by being dragged through the streets alive.

4   TRINITY CHURCH (Broadway at Wall Street)—This has
been one of the richest churches in the world for the past three
centuries. The current church is the third to go up on this site.

In 1705, Queen Anne of England granted the church an
enormous stretch of land going up to Soho, in what became
known as the Great Trinity Land Grab. Descendants of those
who lost land in this transaction fought for over a hundred
years in the courts, but ultimately lost. The church was considered the colonial outpost of England, and even had the right
to unclaimed shipwrecks and all whales that washed up on
shore.

In the 1690s, the church followed a British law that for-
bade the burial of African Americans within its graveyard,
leading to the establishment of the African Burial Ground (see
City Hall Area Tour).

Tenth-anniversary ACT-UP protest, 1997. PHOTO BY ELAINE ANGELOPOULOS

In 1846, when the current structure went up, the church was the tallest building in the city, charging people a fee to climb to the top. By 1857, the church had over $600,000 worth of mortgages on smaller churches and by the early 1990s had rent rolls of $40-$50 million per year, thanks to the land grab. In the 1990s, it underwent an $8 million restoration.

The graveyard predates the church (1681), and holds over eleven hundred bodies, including Alexander Hamilton and Robert Fulton.

Though not a church action, the very first protest of ACT-UP took place in the street in front in March 1987, with over twenty activists getting arrested for blocking traffic. They were protesting pharmaceutical companies' obscene profits from alleged AIDS drugs. ACT-UP has since invaded just about every office in the city and done everything from shut down Grand Central Station during rush hour to interrupting the national evening newscasts.

ACT-UP did a tenth-anniversary follow-up protest on this same corner in March 1997, where seventy-two people were arrested, with one protester viciously beaten up by the police; another common occurrence at ACT-UP protests, along with nasty, homophobic comments.

⑤   NEW YORK STOCK EXCHANGE BUILDING (8 Broad Street)—The New York Stock Exchange started in 1792, when twenty-four merchants, brokers, and auctioneers met under a buttonwood tree in front of 68 Wall Street and agreed to charge one-quarter of one percent commissions for the trading of U.S. bonds. This is the benign way it is described in the textbooks. Today we call it price-fixing. Over one-third of the founders of the exchange were slave-holders—they made money the old-fashioned way; they stole it.

Stockholders get another kind of welfare check; their only labor is in collecting dividend checks each quarter at their mailboxes. (Actually, in most cases, the butler collects the mail.)

There have been many protests at the exchange, especially in the 1960s. In 1966, Youth Against War and Fascism bombarded the trading floor with leaflets condemning the Vietnam War and its corporate supporters. In 1967, the most famous Stock Exchange protest was when Abbie Hoffman and friends, including an unknown Candice Bergen, dumped hundreds of dollar bills onto the trading floor (see East Village II Tour), then danced outside while proclaiming the Death of Money. After this action, a see-through partition was put up to prevent those on the visitor's gallery from doing any more performance pieces.

Abbie Hoffman formed the Yippies (Youth International Party) soon afterwards, a group which inspired another noteworthy 1960s group, WITCH (Women's International Terrorist Conspiracy from Hell). An offshoot of New York Radical Women, on Halloween night in 1968 their first action was to put a hex on the exchange while dressed as witches. They believed in small-scale actions, as opposed to some of the mass actions being organized by other women's groups at the time, when the women's movement was at its height. WITCH also organized an action at Madison Square Garden in 1969, at the annual Bridal Fair; they called women going inside "whores," and released white mice on the floor of the garden.

Other protests at the exchange include the 1979 fiftieth anniversary action of the Wall Street crash that started the Great Depression. Over one thousand people were arrested in an attempt to shut down the exchange, and the day before Daniel Ellsberg burned a dividend check that he had earned just for such an occasion at a rally of two thousand.

In 1989, ACT-UP infiltrated the exchange and interfered with the opening bell by blowing foghorns, urging investors to "Sell Wellcome," a reference to the huge profits the Burroughs Wellcome corporation was making off the highly toxic AIDS drug AZT. Four days later Burroughs Wellcome lowered the price by thirty percent to $5,400 per year.

6   **FEDERAL HALL (28 Wall Street)**—The statue of George Washington in front of this building commemorates the site in 1789 where Washington took the first oath of office to became President of the United States.

On May 8, 1970, more than one thousand students were attacked at a peaceful rally against the Vietnam War and the Pentagon-University connection (see photo on page 105). At noon, two hundred construction workers, acting at the behest of the Republican Party's dirty tricks department, charged into the crowd with pliers and helmets, injuring almost one hundred people, including an aide to then-mayor John Lindsay. While yelling slogans like, "Kill the Commie Bastards," they charged the steps of Federal Hall and draped American flags over the statue of Washington. There were only six arrests, with four police officers injured, as the construction workers ran to City Hall and broke windows at Pace University.

7   **MORGAN GUARANTY TRUST BUILDING (23 Wall Street)**—This building still contains the dynamite marks on

A slave auction, 1845. This image originally ran in *Harper's* magazine with the caption, "The choicest pieces of cargo were sold at auction."
COURTESY OF PHOTOGRAPHS AND PRINTS DIVISION; SHOMBERG CENTER FOR RESEARCH IN BLACK CULTURE; THE NEW YORK PUBLIC LIBRARY; ASTOR, LENOX AND TILDEN FOUNDATIONS

its Wall Street side from a massive explosion on September 16, 1920, which killed thirty-three people and injured four hundred. The New York Chamber of Commerce called it "an act of war," and *The New York Times* devoted its entire front page to it. It caused $2 million worth of damage, and shattered windowpanes as far as one-half of one mile away. It occurred at a time of extreme violence against the working class when killings, deportations, and arrests were reaching an all-time high against Socialists, Communists, anarchists, and labor organizers.

Investigators went to five thousand horse stables, attempting to find the source of the horse and wagon that pulled the explosives up to the bank, but they never solved the case. However, according to anarchist historian Paul Avrich, it was believed to be set by Mario Buda to avenge both the arrest of Sacco and Vanzetti earlier that year, as well as the crackdown against the Italian anarchist community. J.P. Morgan was vacationing in England at the time of the explosion.

8 **CORNER OF WALL STREET AND WATER STREET—** This was the site in 1711 of the Royal African Trading Company, where the British sold and rented enslaved Africans as if they were cattle. Enslaved Africans did all of the essential labor in the British colony of New York, from loading and unloading goods at the docks to piloting boats, building and repairing streets, working the farms, and building colonists' houses.

Though we like to think of the North as a liberal bastion when compared to the South, in the 1770s New York City had the highest percentage of slaves per household than any English colonial settlement except Charleston, South Carolina. New York State was the next-to-last northern state to outlaw slavery in 1827, and many slaves passed through its ports, including through what is now the South Street Seaport—today an overpriced shopping mall—on their way to other destinations.

9 **FRAUNCES TAVERN (54 Pearl Street)**—Built in 1907 as a recreation of the original Fraunces Tavern, this building marks the site of the tavern where a tearful George Washington bade goodbye to his troops after winning the American Revolution.

More interestingly, the tavern was owned by an African American, Samuel Fraunces—a fact always obscured in mainstream history books. Mr. Fraunces' daughter stopped a bodyguard's assassination attempt on George Washington by food poisoning.

More colonial history includes the founding of the U.S. Chamber of Commerce here in 1768 and the meeting where a New York Tea Party was planned against the British in 1774.

The modern radical history involves the famous FALN bombing of the tavern in January 1975, in support of Puerto Rican independence, and in retaliation for a series of bombings against the independence movement in Puerto Rico. The FALN committed over one hundred twenty separate actions from 1974 through 1983, targeting U.S. corporate exploitation of Puerto Rico. This bombing, which actually took place next door at 101 Broad Street, was done specifically to avenge the death of three Puerto Rican Independistas in a restaurant explosion in Mayaguez, Puerto Rico, which also injured ten people.

Puerto Rico has been fighting since 1898 against U.S. control of the island. Its struggle for independence, the loss of lives suffered over the years, makes it one of the bravest struggles for independence of the past one hundred years. In the 1980s, many Puerto Rican Independistas were held at the Metropolitan Correctional Center and vigils supporting them occurred every Sunday evening.

⑩   THE WHITEHALL INDUCTION CENTER (39 State Street)—This 1890s building housed the U.S. Army Induction Center and was replaced by the current New York Health and Racquet Club in 1988. Most of the building was destroyed and replaced by a modern glass monstrosity that passes for architecture these days.

In 1967, Arlo Guthrie immortalized the building in his famous song *Alice's Restaurant Massacre*, wherein he described it as the place where you are "injected, inspected, detected, infected, neglected, and selected."

There have been many demonstrations here over the years, including one sponsored by the League for Sexual Freedom and the Homosexual League, in 1964, against the army's dishonorable discharges of gay men and its failure to guard confidentiality of draft records. This very brave action, in pre-Stonewall-riot America, was composed of ten picketers; the issue unfortunately has not gone away.

In December 1965, sixty-one people were arrested in an anti-war protest while picketing and singing Christmas Carols. A much larger action was during Stop the Draft Week in 1967, when 264 people were arrested in a symbolic civil-disobedience action that was repeated all over the country. Allen Ginsberg and Dr. Benjamin Spock were among the arrestees.

The next day mobile teams engaged in a more militant action in an attempt to physically shut the building, but the twenty-five hundred demonstrators were outnumbered two-to-one by the police and didn't accomplish their task. After regrouping however, marchers shut down rush-hour traffic uptown and forty more demonstrators were arrested. Jerry Rubin, later to be a member of the Chicago seven (or eight, if one includes Bobby Seal) during the 1968 Democratic Convention, was inspired by these mobile battalions, and talked about using it at the convention.

In October 1969, an explosion on the fifth floor shattered forty windows; although it injured no one, it shut down the building for good. It was carried out by John D. Hughey III, a member of the Sam Melville/Jane Alpert group that was immortalized in Ms. Alpert's book *Growing Up Underground*. The communique after the bombing said, "Tonight we bombed the Whitehall Induction Center. This action was in support of the NLF [National Liberation Front of Vietnam], legalized marijuana, love, Cuba, legalized abortion and all of the American revolutionaries and GI's who are winning the war against the Pentagon. Nixon, surrender now."

They continued actions for two years before getting caught by a police informant. Sam Melville worked for the radical

Guardian newspaper, and was active in the 1968 takeover of Columbia University. He was later jailed at Attica prison where he was killed by government SWAT teams as they retook the prison in the famous 1971 hostage-taking incident.

⑪   BATTERY PARK–CASTLE CLINTON—This park was all water before the mid-nineteenth century landfill. It's named for the battery of gun emplacements set up along then-shoreside State Street in the 1690s.

Castle Clinton was a fort built in 1811 to defend New York against the British. From 1855 until 1890, it served as the immigrant landing depot for eight million new arrivals, until it was replaced by Ellis Island. In 1896, it became the New York Aquarium, which was so popular it hosted ninety million people until 1941. It was closed vindictively, however, by New York City Parks Commissioner Robert Moses (see Central Park Tour) and moved to Coney Island, Brooklyn; Moses was furious that his proposal for a bridge from Brooklyn to Battery Park was rejected in favor of the current Brooklyn Battery Tunnel.

Castle Clinton is currently the place where you buy tickets to go to the statue of Liberty and Ellis Island, and it was declared a national monument in 1946.

On the bay side of the fort, there is a magnificent view of New York Harbor. Ellis Island was the inspection point for millions of immigrants from 1892 to 1954, and it is estimated that forty percent of all Americans have a relative who arrived through Ellis Island. Contrary to a very popular myth, not a single person's name was changed at Ellis Island. All passengers gave their names to the boat crew at their point of departure from Europe and this was written down in the boat's manifest in Europe. Upon disembarking at Ellis Island, the manifest was taken out and the passenger identified his or her name—immigrants anglicized their names once in America. Also, two-thirds of all immigrants settled outside of New York City.

When discussing immigration, it is important not to leave out the racist quotas imposed, according to which nationality was perceived as an enemy, or what type of labor was needed at the time. From the Chinese Exclusion Act of 1882 to the 1920s, and the quotas against Southern and Eastern Europeans, America has not always had its arms wide open to "the huddled masses."

Across from Ellis Island stands what became a major symbol of freedom to millions of immigrants coming to America for the first time—the Statue of Liberty. It's ironic that it became associated with the massive European waves of immigrants, because an original model of the statue was a statement against slavery—lady liberty was seen holding a broken vase symbolizing the end of slavery.

It is also ironic that this statue has become so revered; before it was erected in 1886, no one wanted to pay for it. The French gave it to the United States as a gift, but the erection of the base and maintenance was going to cost a lost of money. The U.S. Congress wouldn't spend a penny on it, and for seven years the arm of the statue was displayed in Madison Square Park in New York City and in Philadelphia to drum up support for it.

However, money was not raised in reasonable quantities until 1885, when Joseph Pulitzer, publisher of the *New York World*, promised that anyone who donated as little as a penny would get their name listed on the front page of the newspaper, and over 120,000 Americans responded with contributions totaling $101,000.

In 1986, there was a gala one-hundredth anniversary celebration of the statue featuring President Ronald Reagan, and a laser show on Governor's Island, but there have been much more important events at the statue than these state-sanctioned pageants.

In 1965, for instance, Walter Bowe and three others were arrested for plotting to blow the arms and head off of the statue, along with planned actions at several other patriotic stops

The 1997 protest by Puerto Rican nationalists. © 1997 BY THE NEW YORK TIMES CO. REPRINTED BY PERMISSION.

in the Northeast. They wanted to let the world know that many African Americans did not support the United States Government's genocidal policies against them. They were heavily influenced by the Cuban Revolution and the murder of four African-American children in Birmingham, Alabama in 1963 (see the recent Spike Lee documentary *Four Little Girls* for more about this crime).

In 1971, fifteen members of Vietnam Veterans Against the War occupied the statue for thirty-six hours, and then left with no charges filed against them. In 1974, twenty-one college-age students barricaded themselves inside the statue for fourteen hours. They were members of the Attica Brigade, and demanded the removal of President Nixon—he resigned later that year, although not as a result of the students' demands.

In 1977, thirty Puerto Rican nationalists unfurled a giant Puerto Rican flag, suspended for eight hours, from the statue's crown. In 1980, two people climbed up the statue from the outside with rubber suction cups and hung a twenty-five-foot banner proclaiming "Liberty was framed, Free Geronimo Pratt," referring to the former Black Panther member who was finally released in 1997 after being framed up on a murder charge in Santa Monica, California in December of 1970.

The only action in recent years was the unfurling of two giant banners at the statue in 1991 by Women's Health Action and Mobilization! (WHAM!) to protest the gag rule imposed by President Bush which decreed that abortion could not be mentioned at any health clinic receiving federal funds. WHAM! placed a symbolic gag over lady liberty's mouth, and a giant banner at the base saying "Abortion is Healthcare, Healthcare is a Right." Though the Coast Guard intercepted all boats leaving the island, a small group of activists were able to get away after accomplishing their creative task.

The image of the Statute of Liberty is used in crass advertising campaigns for every type of product, and I end the tour by showing an ad for tampons that proudly showcases the statue, along with several other prominent American historical sites.

The Lower
East Side

PHOTO BY MYRNA KAYTON

The Lower East Side is most famous for its turn-of-the-century Jewish history—from 1881 to 1914, two million Jews fled the Pale of Settlement (the Jewish ghetto of four-five million, which comprised one-third of Russia) to come to the United States. It was the largest movement of Jews in the history of the world up to that time.

Many had been active in the socialist Bund, which unionized the factories and organized political demonstrations against the Czar. They used this experience to found unions in New York City in the garment industry, establish radical newspapers, and elect socialists to office. The Lower East Side spirit is embodied in Emma Goldman, Abraham Cahan, the Rosenbergs, Morris Hillquit and Meyer London—its first Socialist Party congressman.

Peddlers and sweatshops proliferated, as did hundreds of tiny synagogues for the deeply religious orthodox Jews.

There's an old joke about the history of the Jews in New York that says the first generation settled in Manhattan, the second generation moved to the boroughs, the third generation moved to Long Island and Westchester County, and the fourth generation is desperately trying to get an apartment back in Manhattan. Currently three-quarters of the Lower East Side is Latino and Chinese with the remaining twenty-five percent being split between African Americans and Jews, mostly elderly.

LOWER EAST SIDE I TOUR

❶ THE FORMER *JEWISH DAILY FORWARD* BUILDING (175 East Broadway)—This ten-story building was erected in 1911, and became a major center of labor organizing on the Lower East Side (see photo on page 123). Founded in 1897 by Abraham Cahan, *The Forward* grew to a daily circulation of 225,000, the largest circulating Yiddish newspaper in the world. Mr. Cahan was an anarchist, and then a socialist, who gave what is believed to be the first socialist speech in Yiddish in North America in 1882, shortly after his arrival through Castle Garden (see Wall Street Area Tour).

This building was more than simply a newspaper headquarters; it was a center for activism. For boycotts, the paper published lists of companies where workers were on strike, and with the building serving as a strike headquarters.

When Socialist Party Congressman Meyer London won his first election, the results were posted from the windows at two in the morning and thousands gathered in front of a smiling Meyer London, and marched throughout the Lower East Side. When lynchings increased against African Americans in the 1910s, *The Forward* compared them to the pogroms against Jews in Czarist Russia.

The 'Bundle of Letters' column (*Bintel Brief* in Yiddish) fielded questions from the immigrants about this strange new country and its customs, and a collection of letters has since been published in a book that serves as a sociological study of the era. (*A Bintel Brief: Sixty years of letters from the Lower East Side to the Jewish Daily Forward.* [Ballantine, 1971]).

Lower East Side I Tour

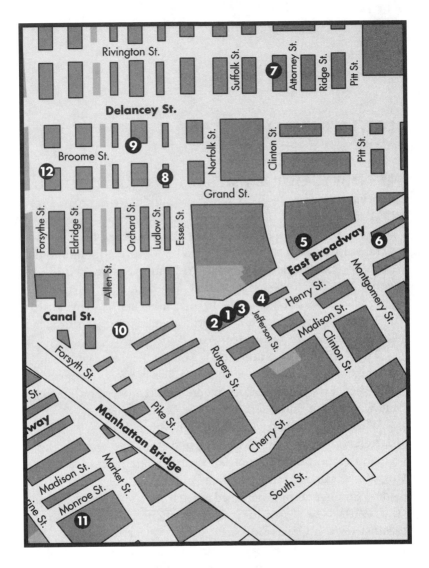

The Forward also published a 'Gallery of Missing Husbands' as poverty forced a desertion rate of ten percent of Jewish husbands; that issue is currently important in the African-American community, with many racists claiming it's the result of something inherent in African Americans.

In 1918, Elizabeth Gurley Flynn, career radical, organized a founding conference of the Workers Liberty Defense Union, which defended members of the IWW, other unions, and radical political party members jailed for their opposition to U.S. entry into WWI. Later, in 1920, she organized the first meeting of the Sacco-Vanzetti Defense Committee, which had representatives from the Socialist Party, Communist Party, and IWW.

The Forward has since moved to the Workmen's Circle Building at 45 East Thirty-third Street, and has become much more conservative. The Chinese church that currently owns the building has literally concealed its radical past. The four large black letters above the four columns on the front cover marble busts of Karl Marx, Frederick Engels, Ferdinand Lasalle (founder of the General Association of German Workers), and Wilhelm Liebknicht (member of the German Social Democratic Party).

This part of East Broadway and Rutgers Street—anchored by the traffic triangle in the center—was called Rutgers Square, but was renamed Strauss Square, for Nathan Strauss, in 1931. He was a partner in R.H. Macy's Department Store, known for his great philanthropy, but also a union buster who, in 1906, fired waitresses organizing at Macy's Department Store in a campaign supported by the Women's Trade Union League (see Lower East Side II and East Village I Tours).

The national head of the Socialist Party, Eugene Debs, held a rally in what was then called Rutgers Square in 1908, during his presidential campaign. In a 1920 election, he received, from jail, over 900,000 votes for president. Had he won, he would have reversed the typical political career trajectory by going to jail *before* assuming office.

2 **THE GARDEN CAFETERIA BUILDING** (165 **East Broadway**)—This Chinese restaurant was the Garden Cafeteria (1911-1983), where one could order a cheap meal, and sit all day arguing over things like socialism versus anarchism, U.S. entry into WWI, or who to support in the upcoming elections. Cafeterias like that dotted New York City, but in recent years most have closed, especially in the midtown Manhattan garment district.

The Workmen's Circle and the *Jewish Daily Forward* held meetings here, and some of the famous people who have eaten here include Isaac Bashevis Singer, Leon Trotsky, and Fidel Castro (Castro lived on West Eight-second Street for several

Site of the old Garden Cafeteria on East Broadway. PHOTO BY BRUCE KAYTON

months in 1949). There was a beautiful "Wall of Respect for Women" mural on the west side of the building next to the subway entrance, but unfortunately it's been painted over and remains a blank white wall today (symbolic of how women's history is treated).

❸   *THE JEWISH DAILY NEWS* BUILDING (185 East Broadway)—This conservative newspaper, stationed along East Broadway, which was then known as the "Yiddish Newspaper Row," is what brought the famous Socialist, Communist, and birth control advocate Rose Pastor Stokes to New York City. Ms. Stokes grew up in England and then Cleveland, Ohio, working ten to eleven hours per day in local factories from the age of eleven. She was one of five children, and her family was so poor that they used to divide the bread up into inch-long pieces. Her father, then stepfather, abandoned the family.

She started to write letters to the *Jewish Daily News* about working-class life in Cleveland. In 1903, they hired her to work for the paper at the salary of $15 per week, and she started her New York City worklife in this building. This poor Jewish girl went on to meet and marry James Graham Phelps Stokes, the millionaire head of the University Settlement (see Lower East Side II Tour) in a marriage that was covered on the front page of *The New York Times*. Ms. Stokes had to quit her factory job at that point because of the publicity, but she joined the Socialist Party, and went on speaking tours for them.

She spoke at a rally at the Bowery and Rivington Street, where over thirty thousand shirtwaist makers were out on strike. Ms. Stokes was a founding member of the Women's Trade Union League, an early member of the National Birth Control League, and later a founding member of what became the American Communist Party. She ran for Congress on the Communist Party line in 1920, was arrested for voting in Greenwich Village in 1918 (see Greenwich Village II Tour), and faced a long prison term for a letter to the editor of a Kansas newspaper opposing U.S. entry into WWI.

She later divorced her millionaire husband and married a union organizer with whom she lived in Chelsea for many years. She finally died of breast cancer in Germany in 1933, where she was receiving radiation therapy. She left $2,000 for a rest home for radicals in her Westport, Connecticut home, but there wasn't enough money to maintain it.

4   EDUCATIONAL ALLIANCE (197 East Broadway)— Before the large Eastern European Jewish immigration wave, a smaller, more economically secure group of German Jews emigrated, landing in New York and many other cities around the country.

These "Uptown Jews" were afraid of an anti-Semitic backlash in response to the immigration of millions of poor Jews. In order to deal with this, the German Jews set up an entire generation of social service agencies and settlement houses to quickly Americanize this "funny-looking, funny-talking, unkempt" group. The Educational Alliance was at the center of this effort, by offering classes in English and typing, dance, art, music, and how to acquire citizenship.

Yiddish was banned at the Educational Alliance for a time, even as Abraham Cahan ran the largest Yiddish newspaper in the world on the next block.

Mark Twain gave readings here, Meyer London took part in English-language political debates, and future blacklisted actor Zero Mostel learned to paint here as a child. Rose Pastor Stokes was the leader of a girl's book club that met here. As was true of many buildings on the Lower East Side at this time, the rooftop was a place for neighborhood residents to hang out and escape the overcrowded streets below.

Across the street at the Seward Park Library (192 East Broadway), a beautiful green cast iron bar adjoins the roof and is a reminder of when the rooftops were major social centers, before television sent everyone to their rooms at night.

Bialystoker home for the aged.
PHOTO BY MYRNA KAYTON

The library went up in 1910, and had long lines of immigrants waiting outside to get in. Currently the most heavily used branch library in New York City is the Flushing Library, serving the Asian community.

⑤ BIALYSTOKER HOME FOR THE AGED (228 and 230 East Broadway)—The taller art deco building was erected in 1932, and the newer annex—now a medical center—went up in 1966. It sports a beautiful, but fading, mural of Jewish life, starting with the immigrants on the boats to the International Ladies Garment Workers Union picketline and the memorial to the holocaust. There are close to 100 senior citizens living here. The home is named for Bialystok, Poland, the home of bialys.

Across the street are rows of small synagogues that still get by, but serve as reminders of the six hundred orthodox synagogues that dotted the Lower East Side at the turn of the century.

⑥ HENRY STREET SETTLEMENT (263, 265, and 267 Henry Street)—Founded in 1893 by Lillian Wald, the Henry Street Settlement has done everything for immigrants from setting up a credit union, offering job counseling, getting doctors in the public schools, building low-cost housing for the community, and getting kids into camp.

Ms. Wald was originally from a rich German Jewish family, but felt very strongly, like *Catholic Worker* founder Dorothy Day, that one should live in the community in which one worked. Ms. Wald's Traveling Nurse Service became a staple on the Lower East Side, with classic pictures of nurses in long dresses jumping from roof to roof to make their rounds. Ms. Wald was an original signer of the call to form the NAACP, and everyone from Theodore Roosevelt to Russian anarchist Peter Kropotkin has visited the settlement.

In 1912, representatives of the Industrial Workers of the World spoke here about the famous Lawrence, Massachusetts "Bread and Roses" strike.

In 1914, Sidney Hillman lived here after being invited by Abraham Cahan to work with the International Ladies Garment Workers Union (ILGWU). Mr. Hillman became a union activist in 1910, during the forty thousand-strong garment worker strike in Chicago against the giant sweatshop company of Hart, Schaffner and Marx. He later worked with the United Garment Workers of America, a conservative AFL union, and took their socialist left-wing into the Amalgamated Clothing Workers of America, which he founded in 1914 (see East Village I Tour).

The mural of Jewish life that adorns the Bialystoker home.
PHOTO BY MYRNA KAYTON

By 1919, the union grew to 138,000 members and Mr. Hillman met Leon Trotsky, Lenin, and endorsed Eugene Debs for president in 1920. In the 1930s, Mr. Hillman was a founding member of the American Labor Party. He became an advisor to New York Governor Lehman and President Franklin Delano Roosevelt.

Hillman was an organizer with the socialist Bund back in Russia, getting arrested in 1904 for leading the first public demonstration of the Bund through the streets of Kovno. He saw himself as a worker first and a Jew second. He spoke with a thick Yiddish accent, and was the target of anti-Semites as a labor advisor for the government.

The Hillman Houses (500, 530 and 550) on Grand Street are named for him and were erected in 1951. After several mergers the Amalgamated Clothing Workers of America are now a part of UNITE!, which was created after a merger with the ILGWU several years ago.

Hillman died in 1946.

7 78 CLINTON STREET—This tenement housed one of the victims of the Triangle Shirtwaist Factory fire of 1911, the horrible sweatshop fire that killed 146 workers, mainly Jewish women between the ages of sixteen and twenty-three (see Greenwich Village I Tour).

The number of people killed was so high that the government didn't have enough coffins on hand. They took the bodies to a dark Twenty-sixth Street pier on the East River and by 7:00 PM that night over two thousand people waited at the gate to identify loved ones who had been killed. Horse-drawn ambulances and police wagons drove up to the gates and deposited bodies inside. By midnight, over 130 bodies had been processed, and the crowd was allowed to enter.

One girl was headless, and others had their clothes burnt off. Some bodies were so badly burnt that they could be identified only through rings and jewelry. Policemen swung lanterns over the bodies in the darkness of the pier and relatives and friends would cry or faint upon identification.

Two neighbors came to the pier five times over three days to identify the body of Julia Rosen of 78 Clinton Street. The police commissioner, due to the fact that a sizable amount of money was found on the body, insisted that a relative be produced before a claim could be made. At 4:30 PM on the afternoon of the third day, fifteen year-old Esther Rosen, Julia's daughter, leaned over the box, touched her head and said that was her mother because she had braided her hair that very day. Esther and her two brothers had waited home all weekend for their mother. The police asked about the money on the body and Esther said that the family came to America four years before but the father had died and Julia always feared leaving the family's savings at home.

As you are crossing Delancey Street, as in the movie title, notice the Williamsburg Bridge. It was erected in 1903 and displaced ten thousand tenants.

8   **SEWARD PARK HIGH SCHOOL (350 Grand Street)**— This 1929 high school sits on the site of the old Ludlow Street Jail (built 1859) and the Essex Street Police Court (built 1856). The jail housed Boss Tweed, the famous corrupt head of the Democratic Party Tammany Hall machine, and he died here in 1878 after being captured in an escape attempt.

The Ludlow Street Jail served as an alimony jail for husbands who deserted their families, and the police court arraigned many of the women who were jailed for picketing during garment industry strikes in the area.

The high school has many famous graduates: Zero Mostel (blacklisted in the 1950s), Jerry Stiller, Walter Matthau, Tony Curtis (then Bernie Schwartz), Moe Biller (president of the American Postal Workers Union in 1980) and Julius and Ethel Rosenberg. The school has a long tradition of serving those whose native language isn't English and this tradition continues today.

❾ LOWER EAST SIDE TENEMENT MUSEUM (90 Orchard Street, (212) 431-0233)—The Tenement Museum offers an excellent tour of the tenement across the street (97 Orchard Street), as well as a video on immigration and New York City history. The museum opened in 1989, in a tenement that went up for $8,000 in the early 1860s. Ten thousand people lived in it until everyone was evicted in 1935 during the depression.

Somewhere on Orchard Street, the 1917 women's food riot started over what was a new phenomenon in American history—inflation. From 1914 to 1920, the cost of living went up over one hundred percent. With people working themselves to death, it seemed impossible to keep one's head above water. Jewish women organized house-to-house boycott campaigns that spread across the Northeast.

It began in Manhattan on February 20, 1917, when famous Lower East Side activist Maria Ganz, who worked as a forewoman in a factory making $10 per week, saw a woman and an onion peddler arguing over food prices on Orchard Street. The peddler was asking for 19 cents per pound, and the woman was arguing with him; the woman, enraged, overturned his cart, and hundreds of women joined in the riot. Fruits and vegetables went flying through the air as the police were called in, only to get pelted with food. The riot spread to nearby Rivington Street, and eventually the women organized a march to City Hall. Maria Ganz was arrested for making a speech in Yiddish; the police admitted they didn't understand it, but claimed its gist was to incite a riot.

A group of women subsequently held a rally at then-Rutgers Square, and set up a committee (The Women's Anti-High Price League) with offices in the *Jewish Daily Forward* building. The League demanded the city buy $1 million worth of food and sell it at cost to the public.

Mayor Mitchell refused to carry out this invasion of the "free market," so the women took up positions at stores and peddler's carts all over the city, boycotting certain foods and making sure anyone who bought them had their baskets over-turned upon exiting from stores. The boycotts were success-ful in causing food to pile up on railroad trains; the price dropped to sell off the surplus.

Food riots occurred in the Bronx and Williamsburg, Brooklyn. Inflation stays with us, as does the legacy of stag-nant wages.

10   ALLEN STREET AND DIVISION STREET—Allen Street is the continuation, southward, of First Avenue. It was originally half as wide, expanded in the 1930s to create a Park Avenue look. It cost $8 million to create this widened street, with $7.6 million going to the real estate industry for the buildings being knocked down. All of the buildings on the east side of Allen Street went up after the 1930s.

The Second Avenue elevated train traveled down the west side of Allen Street, until it was knocked down in 1942. It cost $133,000 to demolish, and it was hoped by storeowners that it would improve sales and the atmosphere of the block. It didn't.

Farther north, between Delancey and Houston Streets, Allen Street was also famous for prostitution. Prostitution was a big industry back in the Pale of Settlement, and it con-tinued on the Lower East Side due to economic exploitation and discrimination. Women could earn $46-$72 per week as a prostitute, as opposed to one-tenth to one-fifth that amount in the local garment industry.

The *Jewish Daily Forward* warned families to stay away from Allen, Chrystie, and Forsythe Streets to avoid the "offi-cial flesh trade in the Jewish quarter."

11   KNICKERBOCKER VILLAGE (10 Monroe Street)—The Rosenbergs lived on the eleventh floor of this building, in an apartment that faced the courtyard, from 1942 to 1950. They were arrested at this address for allegedly selling the secret of the atom bomb in the famous cold war case.

The apartment complex, with sixteen hundred units, was built in 1934 as part of one of Robert Moses' slum clearance projects. It was a joint project of the Metropolitan Life Insurance Company and the federal government. It refused to rent to African Americans through the 1950s.

Ethel Rosenberg never left the Lower East Side until after she graduated high school, growing up in a cold-water flat at 64 Sheriff Street, since knocked down for newer apartment buildings. She was a popular singer at political rallies and a union organizer in the garment district. She met Julius in December 1936, at an International Seaman's Union benefit, when he was with the Young Communist League.

Julius and Ethel Rosenberg were put to death on June 19, 1953. There have been revelations about the case in recent years with the fall of the Soviet Union, but the fact remains that making an atom bomb was not a secret at the time. Also, there is still no evidence that they sold an alleged secret to the Soviet Union, an ally of the United States at the time of the alleged spying. The recent revelations from the Soviet Union via the National Security Agency claim that Julius was a spy and Ethel was not.

At the time of the executions, there were rallies on the Rosenbergs' behalf all over the world, including one on Seventeenth Street off of Union Square in New York City.

⑫   MARX'S FIRST INTERNATIONAL (Empty lot at the corner of Broome and Forsythe Streets, across the street from Sara Delano Roosevelt Park)—The First International, which lasted from 1864 to the mid-1870s, was an attempt to unite the workers of the world. The International Working Men's Association was founded in London, England, with Karl Marx in attendance. It had the following two purposes: 1) To prevent the importation of strikebreakers from one country to another (immigrant labor was brought in for just this purpose in England) and 2) To end wars where workers kill one another for the benefit of rulers.

Anarchist Mikhail Bakunin and Karl Marx got into fights over the centralization of power, and in 1872, the International was moved to this site at what was then the Tenth Ward Hotel, a popular meeting place for Irish and German radicals. Karl Marx felt America was where a worker's organization belonged, because hundreds of thousands of workers were emigrating here every year. He also feared the anarchists would take over the International in Europe.

Section One of the International had its headquarters here under the name "The Communist Club," and there were other sections around New York City as well (Victoria Woodhull, the free-love advocate, headed Section Twelve at 100 Prince Street). There were several more internationals; the Second International, from 1889, was the most successful. It brought together Socialist Parties from around the world, until patriotic aims by individual countries destroyed it during WWI.

Seven blocks of tenements were knocked down to create Sara Delano Roosevelt Park, opened in 1935, then a state-of the-art park, with a large swimming pool, and plenty of breathing room for residents.

Beneath Rivington and Stanton Streets, within the park, was an African burial ground, used after the City Hall area burial ground was full (1795 to 1853). In the 1970s and 1980s, it was known as New York City's largest open-air heroin market, but it has since improved, featuring sports and free outdoor movies.

To continue a long tradition, as well as a radical walking tour tradition, end your walk with a meal at Katz's Delicatessen at the corner of Houston and Ludlow Streets. It has been here since 1888, makes twelve thousand hot dogs a week, and recreates the old "Garden Cafeteria" atmosphere.

LOWER EAST SIDE II TOUR

① **SEWARD PARK LIBRARY** (192 East Broadway)—On the east wall of the library is the imprint of an older tenement, part of a block-long row. It included halls, rented out by radicals for lectures and organizing meetings. Anarchist Emma Goldman lectured here. One of the missing tenements housed Morris Hillquit's law practice, at 198 East Broadway; Mr. Hillquit decided to keep in touch with his Lower East Side roots after running a successful uptown practice. He was the head of the Socialist Party in New York City. His unsuccessful runs for office paved the way for the successful campaigns of Congressman Meyer London.

After coming to America in 1886, Hillquit worked in the United Hebrew Trades and the Socialist Labor Party at their headquarters at 25 East Fourth Street. He settled down on Clinton Street, worked with Abraham Cahan on the *Arbeiter Zeitung* (Worker's Paper) before the *Jewish Daily Forward* was born, and was a founding member of the national Socialist Party, after it broke away from Daniel DeLeon's Socialist Labor Party.

Though he lost the 1917 mayoral election, he won twenty-two percent of the vote, and his activism on behalf of women's suffrage enabled a referendum to pass giving women the vote in New York State the following year. He defended *The Masses* during its first trial for violation of the Espionage Act in 1918, earning a hung jury. He represented the ILGWU, and notorious anarchist Johann Most (see East Village II Tour)

Lower East Side II Tour

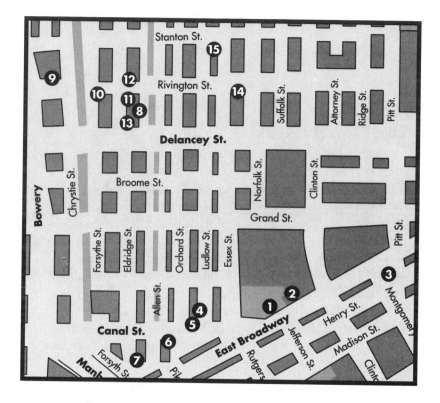

in 1901 after Most was wrongfully charged with inspiring the murder of President McKinley. He died of tuberculosis in 1933 at the age of sixty-four.

The Seward Park Housing Complex, adjoined to the site, went up in 1967, and actually two generations of tenements have been knocked down since 1900. Seward Park, on the west side of the library, was built in 1900, and named for Governor William Seward of New York.

② HOME OF ANARCHIST AND IWW ORGANIZER SAM DOLGOFF (208 East Broadway)—Sam Dolgoff was a great old anarchist who died in 1990 while living in the Seward Park housing complex, where the rents had been kept low until recently, when apartments were put up for sale.

Sam represents the many organizers, not world-famous, who gave their lives to the movement. He was an unforgettable character. Born in Russia, he came here illegally, and first joined the Socialist Party before finding it too reformist. He got involved in an anarchist publication called *Road to Freedom*, from 1924 to 1932, and then another anarchist magazine called *Vanguard*.

He developed a lifelong friendship with anarchist Carlo Tresca (see East Village I and Chelsea–Ladies' Mile Tours), traveled all over the country on speaking and union-organizing trips, and was active with the anarchist Modern School when it moved to Stelton, New Jersey (see East Village I Tour). He wrote books and pamphlets on the Spanish Revolution, a critique of the Cuban Revolution, and stood up to many people as a soapbox orator in the street.

Once, a man derided Sam's anti-war stance by saying that he proudly sent his son to war. Sam answered: "You would send your son to war? Even a rat protects its young." His apartment was always open for young people to drop in, including this author, and he was always provocative and interesting.

His knowledge of history was vast and yet, on occasion, when I would ask him questions about a historical landmark or specific event, he would answer, "Who the hell cares about that old thing?" His comrade and wife, Esther, who died in 1989, would usually answer, "What do you mean? He wants to know."

When he died a memorial, which attracted several hundred people from many different areas of his life, was held at the old Village Gate on Bleecker Street.

❸   275 EAST BROADWAY (Now the middle of the road at center of Pitt Street)—Meyer London lived in a house at this address before Pitt Street was paved through, creating a large open-air space non-existent at the turn of the century. He was born in a Russian-Polish province in 1871, and came to the United States in 1888. Originally a Socialist Labor Party (SLP) member, he left the party in opposition to Daniel DeLeon, and joined the Socialist Party, which opposed and splintered from the SLP.

He served as a lawyer to many of the garment unions on the Lower East Side, and helped put together the 1910 Protocol of Peace Agreement that served as a model for unions for the rest of the century. In 1914, he was elected the first Socialist Party Congressmen, winning forty-seven percent of the vote. He led a rally in front of the *Jewish Daily Forward* Building at 4:00 AM that night (see Lower East Side I Tour).

He served two more terms in Congress, but finally lost in 1922 to Democratic Party hack Samuel Dickstein, after the Democrats and Republicans worked together to gerrymander the district, a common practice to keep Socialists out of office. The street sign facing what was Meyer London's house names the plaza for Samuel Dickstein, an unfortunate decision that further insults democratic principles. Meyer London died in 1926, after getting hit by a taxicab. He had spent his entire life on the Lower East Side; hundreds of thousands lined the streets for his funeral procession.

4 THE INDEPENDENT KLETZKER BROTHERLY AID ASSOCIATION BUILDING (5 Ludlow Street)—This building went up in 1910, and served as a *landsmanschaft* for immigrants from the Polish village of Kletsky. A *landsmanschaft* is the place where new immigrants from a particular town go in order to have a social base from which to operate since their townsmen have already settled there.

Today, it is a funeral home, serving both the chinese and italian communities, with a separate entrance for each. The upper stories once were a synagogue and are now co-op apartments.

5 45 CANAL STREET—This address, though probably not the same building, is where a young twenty year-old Russian-Jewish woman stayed during her first week in New York City. Emma Goldman couldn't wait to escape the oppression of Rochester, New York, where her orthodox father from Russia and first husband were.

She took the ferry from Weehawken, New Jersey on August 15, 1889 to Forty-second Street in Manhattan. She hadn't imagined Manhattan that large and ended up carrying her bags for three hours in the hot summer sun before finding her aunt and uncle's photography studio and apartment at 45 Canal Street.

In a continuing tradition of Jewish family relations, upon her arrival Emma was asked a million questions. She quickly moved out, meeting Alexander Berkman at Sach's Cafe on Suffolk Street soon after. She worked in sweatshops in the area and supported the 1890 Tailor's Strike (see below).

6 FORMER JARMULOVSKY BANK BUILDING (54-58 Canal Street)—Sender Jarmulovsky came from Russia and opened a bank in the 1870s on Canal and Orchard Streets. He survived several bank runs, and in 1912, with a view to a lucrative future, he paid to have this building built. He died before it was completed, but his sons took over, only to see the bank go under in 1917 during WWI, when depositors with-

The Jarmulovsky Bank site. PHOTO BY MYRNA KAYTON

drew their money en masse to send it to relatives in Europe. One of the sons was attacked by a depositor with a knife and there were riots here as well. In September 1914, five hundred people who lost their hard-earned money gathered in front of the bank and the Jarmulovsky children had to flee via the roof. In 1914, fifty thousand working people lost $10 million, with six committing suicide.

❼   ELDRIDGE STREET SYNAGOGUE (12-14 Eldridge Street)—The first synagogue built by the Jews of the Lower East Side (1887), the inspiration to erect it came largely from pride in relation to the uptown Jews, who had been here longer, and were wealthier. It cost $100,000 to build. They charged $1,000 for sanctuary seats in the front of the temple during the high holy days.

Sender Jarmulovsky was the president of the congregation, eventually abandoned by the 1950s when there weren't enough Jews left to keep it alive. It is now open for tours on Sundays and in the midst of an $8 million renovation campaign.

Across the street are a variety of employment agencies, continuing around the corner. Many of these sweatshop employment agencies are a part of the vast exploitation network that continues a horrible tradition from the turn of the century; the ethnicity of the workers has changed from Jewish to Chinese.

Dozens of Chinese employment agencies hire undocumented workers for slave wages, usually workers from the seaport village of Fuzhou in the Republic of China. They pay over $30,000 to get smuggled to America and then work six or seven-day weeks, eighteen hours a day, at below-minimum wages, to pay back their debt.

They sleep in shifts in rooms with over twenty people, and if they are not paying back their debt fast enough they could be threatened, killed, or kidnapped. It's estimated that fifty to one hundred fifty thousand workers are in this predicament as the United States economy continues its dependence on massive exploitation of the working class.

The plight of Chinese immigrants was highlighted in 1993, when the ship Golden Venture ran aground in Rockaway, Queens carrying 286 immigrants, ten of whom died trying to swim ashore. Some of them had been on the ship for a year trying to get to America. Many were jailed for years until a wave of releases in 1996 and 1997.

8 **FORMER ALLEN STREET BATHS (133 Allen Street)**— This former public bath building operated from 1905 to 1988 before being sold by the city in a public auction in 1992. Public baths were extremely important to the city when early tenements were predominantly cold-water flats.

At the turn of the century, there were twenty-five public baths in New York City. Later, the city erected fifteen floating docks for swimming in the East and Hudson Rivers.

The Allen Street Baths were used by thirty thousand people per year as late as the 1970s, and it is estimated over four million people bathed here over its history.

⑨   8 RIVINGTON STREET—This was the tenement where the Biermans lived, whose daughter Gussie was one of the victims of the Triangle Shirtwaist Factory fire. When the Biermans went to the Twenty-sixth Street Pier on the East River to identify the body, they noticed she had been stripped of three rings, a watch, a chain, and earrings. She had also kept her cash in her shoe, but that too was missing.

The alley next to the building is classic turn-of-the-century. The nearby corner of the Bowery and Rivington Streets was where Rose Pastor Stokes spoke in 1910 to thirty thousand striking garment workers.

⑩   RIVINGTON HOUSE (45 Rivington Street)—This 1890s school building is now a 219-bed AIDS facility that opened in 1995 after a six-year renovation effort. It has four hundred employees, and a $25 million budget. Probably the most famous person to die here was Terry Miller, who wrote the magnificent book on Greenwich Village called "Greenwich Village and How It Got That Way," which is still in print.

⑪   UNIVERSITY SETTLEMENT (184 Eldridge Street)—The oldest settlement house in the United States was founded in 1886 at a different site, but built this 1898 building for $200,000 and made it its headquarters. Millionaire James Graham Phelps Stokes ran it for many years (see Rose Pastor Stokes in the Lower East Side I Tour) and it would establish a library for prisoners at the Tombs downtown, lobby for tenement reform, give strikers free meals, and charge bathers merely a nickel to use its basement showers. Settlement members lobbied for a municipal subway system, the creation of public bathhouses, and gave classes in English and recreational programs for children.

The Women's Trade Union League (WTUL) had early meetings here in 1905, as well as their May Day Dance in 1908. The WTUL had chapters around the east coast in order to get more women into unions and to fight for labor legislation. The WTUL organized at the Triangle Shirtwaist Factory in 1909, and then inserted questionnaires in the major newspapers on fire safety after the 1911 tragedy.

The League was class-integrated with richer, middle-class women giving financial support to working-class organizers on the picket lines. Its most prominent members included Rose Schneiderman, Mary Drier, Ida Rauh, and Leonora O'Reilly.

⑫ 192 ELDRIDGE STREET AND THE 1890 CLOAK-MAKER'S AND TAILOR'S STRIKE—Sweatshops existed all over the city, and wages were continually driven downward by the surplus in labor, as the sweatshop contractors all competed with each other to make garments for less and less money in order to win jobs from larger manufacturers.

On July 3, 1890, cloakmakers and tailors were locked out by their employers during a unionization drive. The workers, mainly Russian and Polish Jews, beat up some scabs on Lower Broadway. The most serious action of the strike, however, took place on the top floor of this tenement where Samuel Billett, a Russian-Jewish contractor, lived with his wife and five children. He kept his shop/home open during the strike, where he employed eight men and one girl in a large room on the Rivington Street side of the tenement.

At 11 AM, a group of striking workers left Pythagors Hall on Canal Street with shears and cutting knives. The crowd grew to two hundred as they approached the tenement. They rushed up the stairway, tore through the locked door, and destroyed over $200 worth of cloth, threw Mr. Billet to the ground and beat him along with the other scabs. Billet took out a gun and shot one of the strikers, Abraham Rosenberg, causing serious injury.

A police officer came running in after hearing the shots, and held eight strikers before police reinforcements from the Eldridge Street Police Precinct arrived. The eight men were captured and arraigned at the Essex Street Police Court (see Lower East Side I Tour) and charged with burglary and assault. Mr. Billet was charged with felonious assault but, unlike the strikers, was released because he could make bail.

The strike was symbolic of the hard battle that had to be fought for the very rights we take for granted today, like the eight-hour day. It lasted nine weeks and ended in victory for the workers. Joseph Barondess, an early Jewish labor leader, became famous through this strike and led a victory parade. The tireless Emma Goldman also worked on the strike.

⓭   WORKMEN'S CIRCLE (174 Eldridge Street)—This tenement housed Hyman Levy in 1892, a tailor and early member. Some of the earliest meetings of the Workmen's Circle were held here. The first Workmen's Circle meeting was at 151 Essex Street, in March 1892 at cloakmaker Sam Greenberg's apartment).

The Workmen's Circle was a combination social-service center and socialist training ground. It offered health and welfare services, funeral benefits, lectures on Socialism, and support for the Sacco-Vanzetti Fund, the Triangle Shirtwaist Factory victims, and A. Philip Randolph's Socialist magazine, *The Messenger.*

By 1925, the Circle had eighty-five thousand members. They closed on International Workers Day and the anniversary of the Russian Revolution, but remained open on Jewish holidays. They had a large network of schools and summer camps, but are currently much smaller with an excellent bookstore at their headquarters at 45 East Thirty-third Street.

The membership today stands at thirty thousand members nationwide.

⓮   123 AND 125 RIVINGTON STREET—One twenty-three Rivington Street is the address that Meredith Tax used for the Jewish family in her magnificent novel *Rivington Street.* They leave Russia for America after the Kishiniev pogrom. Tax deals with topics such as Socialism, Communism, union organizing, lesbians, and other aspects of life on the Lower East Side. Written in the tradition of an Upton Sinclair-style political novel, it remains in print along with its sequel, *Union Square.*

One hundred twenty-five Rivington Street was known as Eisler's Golden Rule Hall. In the 1890s, it hosted five separate congregations worshipping on its five separate floors, but it was also an important meeting place for union organizers and radicals.

In June of 1882, hundreds of Jews, as was commonly practiced, sat on the grass near Castle Garden in Battery Park, waiting to be picked for work in what was known as the "Shape-up." Five hundred were hired to work on the docks farther upriver, but they found out after two days on the job that they were being used as scabs against the Irish dockworkers. A meeting was called, and the Jewish dockworkers got their money ($3 instead of the $6 they were promised), and joined the Irish strikers. Five thousand workers marched from Battery Park to Union Square, with the German Social-Democrats speaking to Jewish immigrants at Battery Park about forming an organization and attracting Russian Jews to the movement.

The first meeting was held at Eisler's Golden Rule Hall, and a young man named Abraham Cahan (see Lower East Side Tour I), a cigar factory worker, attended. More than five hundred people squeezed into chairs and leaned against the walls, with Mr. Cahan complaining at the end of the meeting that Yiddish should be spoken too. The organizers agreed, and shortly afterward Cahan gave, in a beer saloon on East Sixth Street, what is believed to be the first Yiddish-language Socialist speech ever delivered in North America. Mr. Cahan went on to become a freelance journalist, formed several Russian worker organizations, and finally, founded the *Jewish Daily Forward* in 1897.

One hundred twenty-five Rivington Street is also the address of African Free School #4. There were over a dozen

African Free Schools in lower Manhattan from 1787 to 1834 in order to educate soon-to-be-free African slaves (see Greenwich Village II Tour).

⑮   JACOB JAVITS'S BIRTHPLACE (85 Stanton Street)— Former U.S. Senator Jacob Javits was born in this tenement in 1904, where his father worked as the superintendent. His mother sold dry goods from a pushcart in the street to help make ends meet. A liberal Republican who lost to the long-corrupt Senator Alphonse D'Amato in 1980, Mr. Javits helped pass ERISA (which guarantees private pension plans) and establish the National Endowment for the Arts and the Humanities. He died in 1986, but not before having the Jacob Javits Convention Center named after him.

City Hall

PHOTO BY PETER JOSEPH

The City Hall area is dominated by imposing government buildings erected with government money. But there are other, privately-owned office and apartment buildings, put-up also with government money, in the form of vast subsidies and tax breaks.

There are interesting statistics on our one-of-a-kind city which should be revealed while one gazes upon City Hall. If New York City were a state, its $31 billion budget would place it among the top five *state* budgets in the country. The New York City Government electric bill is $250 million. There are over three million jobs in New York City, $2.7 trillion in real estate, one million children in school, and officially 7.3 million people overall.

There are tens of thousands of homeless people and the city has lost over 750,000 manufacturing jobs from the late 1950s through the early 1990s. There are currently thirty-eight thousand police officers, with complaints of police brutality becoming a major concern of activists under New York City's 107th Mayor, Rudolph Giuliani.

There are over fifty million square feet of empty office space, and due to a lack of jobs, over nine hundred thousand receiving welfare benefits. Crime is down significantly and, contrary to popular wisdom, New York City is now the safest city in the United States with a population over one million.

CITY HALL AREA TOUR

1 CITY HALL—Completed in 1811 at a cost of $500,000, this was the third City Hall in New York City (see photo on page 151). The population at that time was only one hundred thousand, and the building looked out on the harbor from the top of this hill, a view that disappeared a long time ago due to skyscraper construction.

City Hall Park was New York City's first official park, and its use as a commons goes back to 1686. In 1776, the Declaration of Independence was read here to colonial troops and citizens in the presence of George Washington, though most of the people in the colony were not free.

There's an old saying that you can't fight City Hall, but history refutes this. In 1826 and 1832, there were major riots against hearings to determine if certain African Americans were runaway slaves who should be sent back to southern slaveowners. In 1826, a crowd of African Americans amassed in the park and bombarded the slave catcher with bricks, sticks and stones. One police officer was hit with a brick, several were arrested, and rioting continued on Ann Street.

1837 saw the famous flour riot, where six thousand assembled to protest the price increase from $6 to $15 per barrel. One of the speakers mentioned that Eli Hart and Company was nearby (the site now adjacent to the World Trade Center) and that they had fifty-three barrels of flour waiting inside. The crowd took the hint, overpowered the police, and thousands of barrels of flour were liberated and/or spilled all over

City Hall Area Tour

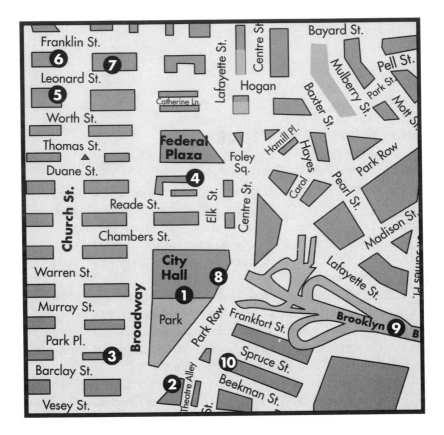

the street. The rioting went on for hours and forty people were convicted of rioting and sentenced to Sing Sing Prison.

The other big riot, which took place right on the steps of City Hall, occurred in 1857, when New York City had two competing police departments. One was from the state, designed to clean up corruption and the other was the city police force. Mayor Fernando Wood refused to follow the orders of the governor, and would eventually cause a riot by throwing out the warrant server who was going to arrest him.

Hand-to-hand combat ensued as the police clubbed each other, broke each other's skulls, and threw each other down the steps of City Hall. The State Police were defeated with one officer becoming permanently crippled, but then the National Guard's Seventh Regiment was sent in.

They were marching down Broadway to the docks at the time to take a boat, ironically, to a celebration in Boston of the Battle of Bunker Hill. The mayor was arrested, and ultimately the state police replaced the city police, throwing eleven hundred men out of work during a depression.

The lawless activity brings to mind the 1992 police riot at City Hall, when ten thousand officers marched against Mayor Dinkins' proposed reform of the Civilian Complaint Review Board (considered a joke today). They used racial epithets against New York City's first African-American Mayor, damaged cars, charged up the steps of City Hall, and later blocked traffic on the approach to the Brooklyn Bridge for forty-five minutes—certainly a tactic they learned through their infiltration of ACT-UP meetings and demonstrations.

They called Councilwoman Una Clarke a "nigger," and wouldn't let her cross into City Hall. They nearly beat to death an African-American man in the subway after the protest. Then-mayoral candidate Rudolph Guiliani was speaking at the police officer's rally and using words that can't be printed in a family publication.

Two opposing Vietnam War demonstrations took place on consecutive days at City Hall in May 1970. The first featured sixty thousand construction workers, paid to attend in order to show support for President Nixon and his "Silent Majority." (Nixon claimed the majority of Americans supported him but they just weren't out in the streets proclaiming it, like his opponents.) The next day, twenty thousand anti-Vietnam War protesters rallied at City Hall, with one thousand marching to midtown before being violently stopped by the police at Thirty-ninth Street, injuring nine.

In 1988, there was a homeless encampment at City Hall Park for fifty days in order to embarrass the politicians inside City Hall who were cutting the housing budget. It started with a rally of four hundred and those in attendance decided, with no home to go to afterwards, that they may as well stay right in the park.

They organized themselves into a group called "Homeward Bound," set up informational tables, food distribution, and kept the park cleaner than it has ever been. They named the camp "Kochville," after Mayor Koch, continuing a tradition of "Hoovervilles" and "Dinkinsvilles" in New York City.

In the 1890s, author Jack London lived as a hobo in City Hall Park, sleeping and eating here until he was attacked by clubwielding policemen. He later wrote classics such as *The Iron Heel* and *Call of the Wild*.

On July 3, 1989, there was a women's demonstration against the Supreme Court's restrictive Webster decision on abortion. A crowd of two thousand, predominantly women, took over Centre and Chambers Streets, as well as the approach to the Brooklyn Bridge, before twenty people got arrested doing civil disobedience on Park Row. Out of this demonstration, and the Webster decision, the Reproductive Rights Coalition (RRC) formed, which drew over five hundred people to its early weekly meetings. Out of RRC grew WHAM!, which staged dozens of demonstrations throughout Manhattan in the early 1990s, as well as abortion-clinic defense (see Wall Street Area Tour).

The fountain at the southern tip of the park marks the

spot where the old post office building stood, until it was knocked down in 1938. It was an imposing building, which interfered with the park and was hated, except by the corrupt Boss Tweed (see below), who made a pretty penny through its construction.

It's noteworthy, though, because it is where the 1918 *Masses* magazine trial took place, the editors and staff being charged with violation of the Espionage Act for opposing U.S. entry into WWI. The trial, with Morris Hillquit defending the staff, ended in a hung jury, thanks to one jurist who held out. The defendants were able to see the jury deliberations at night in the reflection of the Woolworth Building.

② **15 PARK ROW**—This was the tallest building in the world when completed in 1899. It housed the Bureau of Investigation in 1920, which ties it into the Sacco-Vanzetti case (the two Italian anarchists executed in 1927 for a robbery and murder in South Braintree, Massachusetts).

Sacco and Vanzetti were part of a group of Italian anarchists who did intensive political work in anticipation of a true American Revolution. They also supported bombings and warfare against the capitalists and the government. One of their main organizers was Luigi Galleani, the editor of *The Subversive Chronicle*, which published for over fifteen years.

Galleani was arrested a number of times, finally being deported in 1919, due to his political beliefs, under the Alien Exclusion Act. This enraged his supporters all over the country, who responded with bombings.

On the fourteenth floor of this building, at the Bureau of Investigation's office, Roberto Elia, a printer, was held for eight weeks because his paper was found to be similar to the paper used on communiques after bombings over the previous two years. Elia heard cries of pain from the next room, and he recognized his fellow employee, Andrea Salsedo.

Salsedo also worked at *The Subversive Chronicle*, and was beaten up during his interrogation. The two of them admitted to printing some of the communiqués, and they anticipated deportation. However, they continued to be held illegally.

They were asked to identify photographs of other anarchists, which they did. In March 1920, Salsedo was able to smuggle a note to Vanzetti, asking for money and explaining what had happened. Vanzetti raised money in East Boston, and tried to get Salsedo a better lawyer. He made a trip to Manhattan to see Salsedo but wasn't able to get in.

Salsedo became increasingly despondent, and on May 2, 1920, he jumped to his death from the fourteenth floor. His wife sued the city for $100,000, but lost the case and returned to Italy. Elia was later deported, continuing his political work there.

Sacco and Vanzetti were arrested in 1920, while making plans to leave for Italy, and executed seven years later, after one of the most watched trials of the century.

Galleani was charged with sedition in Mussolini's Italy, served fourteen months, and died in 1931 after serving two more prison terms.

❸   THE NEW YORK CALL (6 Park Place, now the site of the Woolworth Building)—This was the site of the offices of the Socialist newspaper, *The New York Call*. The newspaper was founded in 1908 as a small weekly, published by the Workingmen's Co-Operative Publishing Association, which had previously worked with the Socialist Labor Party.

It sat across City Hall Park from the mainstream "Newspaper Row," on Park Row, had a circulation of twenty-three thousand, which was about one tenth that of the major mainstream newspapers. It published at a time, in the 1910s, when the Socialist Party was at its height, and the number-one circulating magazine in the country was the Socialist *Appeal to Reason* with a circulation of 750,000.

Rose Pastor Stokes and Margaret Sanger wrote for *The New York Call*, and it had the best coverage of the Triangle Shirtwaist Factory fire of 1911; they, in fact, were offered a

$250 bribe from the owners of the factory to stop reporting on the fire.

The Woolworth Building that stands on this spot now was the tallest building in the world when it went up in 1913 at a cost of $13.5 million. Woolworth's was founded in 1879, and will go down in history for the sit-ins and protests that occurred on its premises during the Civil Rights movement of the 1960s.

You can't talk about New York City without mentioning the word corruption. The king of corruption was William Marcy Boss Tweed, the head of the Democratic Party (Tammany Hall was the headquarters) in the latter half of the nineteenth century (see Lower East Side Tour).

He eventually died in jail, after stealing an estimated $30 million, but a monument to his greed still stands: the "Old Tweed Courthouse" sits at 52 Chambers Street between Broadway and Centre Street, yet another nondescript marble building in the area.

It cost $16 million to build in 1878, with an estimated $10 million going for payoffs. Items were billed at outrageous rates during its construction, such as $41,000 for brooms and $8,000 for each window.

4 **THE AFRICAN BURIAL GROUND (Corner of Duane and Elk Streets)**—This small grass plot is all that was salvaged of the African Burial Ground, which is believed to stretch to Broadway and as far south as Chambers Street. It is estimated that twenty thousand bodies are buried here, in what was considered useless land when it was a burial ground from the 1710s to the 1790s.

It was "discovered" when the foundation for the building at 290 Broadway was being dug in 1991, leading to protests and memorials to preserve it, and study the 427 exhumed bodies. The federal government was more concerned with finishing its $276 million project than in giving African slaves their proper respect. Politicians and organizers such as Mayor

David Dinkins, Congressman Gus Savage, Elombe Brath, and Sonny Carson enabled the bodies to be preserved, and they are currently being studied at Howard University.

In 1991, there was a twenty-six hour vigil of drumming, speeches, and religious ceremonies, with the drummers saying over and over "They can steal the drums, but they can't steal the beat, they can steal the drums, but they can't steal the best."

The grass area was to be covered by a pavilion, but thanks to community protest it will be preserved as a burial ground.

Children's skeletons were found with bad cavities, a sign of poor nutrition, and many of the skeletons contain deformities from the horror of a life spent in slavery. Almost all of the coffins had long since dissolved over time, but five stone markers were found and one body had a musket ball in its rib cage. Many artifacts from Africa were found adorning the bodies as well.

The current Liaison Office on the African Burial Ground can be reached at (212) 264-0424, for more information and tours of the artifacts. The bodies being studied are expected to be re-interred in the year 2000, and it is also long past due that an African Holocaust Museum be built in New York City.

❺   SITE OF MOTHER AME ZION CHURCH (Plaque in sidewalk on southwest corner of Church and Leonard Streets)—The history of African-American churches in the United States began with Reverend Richard Allen, and the Bethel AME Church in Philadelphia. Reverend Allen was a former slave who gave services to a predominantly white church at St. George's. He decided African Americans needed their own church after a group was thrown out of the white section of a segregated church in 1793.

Reverend Absalom Jones was later commissioned to go to New York and set up a branch of the AME Church in New York, which he did in the 1810s, in a schoolroom on Mott Street.

Plaque commemorating the site of AME Zion Church. PHOTO BY PETER JOSEPH

While the Philadelphia African-American church was being erected in 1796, Peter Williams, an ex-slave and sexton formed, along with the predominantly white John Street Methodist Church, the Mother AME Zion Church in New York City. It opened in 1800 and, it progressed from a stable, to a stone building, to a brick building in 1840.

In 1829, Isabella, an escaped slave, renounced her slave name in the pulpit of this church and took the name Sojourner Truth. She lived in New York City from 1829 to 1844, and led over one thousand slaves to their freedom.

Frederick Douglass, the great speaker, writer, and anti-slavery activist, was married in New York City, and was a preacher with the AME Zion Church in New Bedford, Massachusetts.

By the 1920s, all the major African-American churches had moved from midtown Manhattan to Harlem, where they remain today.

6 **SITE OF *FREEDOM'S JOURNAL* HEADQUARTERS (250 Church Street)**—This was the site of the first African-

American newspaper in America, published in 1828 by Samuel Cornish and John Russworm. Russworm was one of the first African Americans to graduate from an American college. He supported the Back-to-Africa Movement through the American Colonization Society, which later formed the country of Liberia. New York State has always had many African-American newspapers; the most famous of the nineteenth century being Frederick Douglass' *North Star*.

❼ 79 LEONARD STREET—The basement of this building was the home of the Marxist School in the late 1980s and early 1990s, where one could rub shoulders with Morton Sobell, Bertell Ollman, and Annette T. Rubinstein. They also offered great Radical Walking Tours in the 1980s—conducted by Gene Glickman—and the author continued this tradition in the 1990s.

Started in 1979, the school has offered excellent lectures, movies, and classes over the years. They can be reached at their current location (122 West Twenty-seventh Street, Tenth Floor) at (212) 242-4201.

In the late 1980s and early 1990s, on the main floor, the Socialist Workers Party gave lectures and had a bookstore.

❽ THE HISTORY OF THE SUBWAYS (City Hall subway stop with the kiosk below Chambers Street adjoining the Brooklyn Bridge)—The first subway started at City Hall, followed the Lexington Avenue Line to Forty-second Street, went westward, then followed the current "3" train route, to 145th Street in Manhattan. Tax dollars paid to build the subway, but private companies leased, equipped, and operated the lines. The executives gave themselves large salaries, and stockholders made a killing, while very little money went into workers' salaries or maintenance, something we're paying for today. By 1930, the three major subway and railway companies had total assets of $850 billion. The subways also doubled real estate values in the city.

Company unions and union-busting were the order of the day in the subways until the Transport Workers Union was formed in 1934. It was formed by a combination of the Communist Party, and militant Irish workers who had gotten their early organizing experience with the Irish Republican Army in Ireland. The fight to unionize the subways was rough and violent, including a brawl in front of Grand Central Station in 1935 involving two hundred people during an attempt to arrest Mike Quill, a union founder.

Currently, there are over seven hundred miles of subway track, over 930 toilets, and 1.5 million light bulbs.

New York City has the least subsidized subway system in the country. By 1990, there were one billion passenger trips per year, which was just half the total during the WWII boom. Besides the initial lack of money going to repair and modernize the subways, Robert Moses (see Central Park Tour) spent very little money on them; he was subsidizing the car culture and the growth of suburbia through massive bridge, tunnel, and parkway construction from the 1920s to the 1960s.

❾   THE BROOKLYN BRIDGE (you can walk onto the bridge at the center path on Centre Street in front of the Municipal Building at 1 Centre Street)—This was one of the great wonders of the world upon completion in 1883, at a height more than double the size of any bridge previously built. As with many New York City construction projects, it included massive corruption, union-busting, and horrible conditions for the workers.

The ubiquitous Boss Tweed was one of six members of the Executive Committee of the Bridge Company, and though Brooklyn and Manhattan financed ninety percent of the cost of the bridge, it was private stockholders who had control. Because the private sector was not monitored, one of the contractors, Kingsley and Keeney, was actually commended for their restraint in only stealing $125,000 through false billings.

Between twenty to forty workers died building the bridge. One-third of the European immigrant laborers quit each week due to the difficulty of work underneath the water in the giant caissons upon which the towers rest.

Workers developed the bends, bronchitis, hacking coughs and severe colds. When three workers died in May 1872, the entire caisson work force went on strike. They demanded $3 per day for four hours of work before the contractor, Mr. Kingsley, threatened to fire everyone who didn't return to work. The workers caved-in.

The bridge took fourteen years to complete and is held up by fourteen thousand miles of wire, and ultimately cost $15 million to complete. Eight years after construction it was found that a cheaper wire had been substituted by the contractor J. Lloyd Haigh, but since the specifications were stringent, it was felt the bridge would last anyway. The wire has held up, though a $9 million renovation in 1948 ensured it would last another century or two.

The bridge led to the incorporation of Brooklyn into New York City in 1898, as its population went from three thousand residents in 1810 to one million in the 1890s. Its natural stone towers are a striking contrast to the steel structures of the Manhattan Bridge and all subsequent bridges. A walk across, which is a little over one mile, brings you into beautiful Brooklyn Heights and its promenade, offering a great view of Manhattan.

⑩   SITE OF *NEW YORK TRIBUNE* (corner of Spruce and Nassau Streets)—The most important newspaper in the United States in the mid-nineteenth century, with a circulation of 200,000, was the *New York Tribune*. Horace Greeley, the publisher, was an outspoken opponent of slavery who hired, as a foreign correspondent, the very first Marxist, Karl Marx. He was the London correspondent from 1851 to 1861; Frederick Engels wrote many of the articles for him, giving

Marx more time for theoretical work. It took two weeks for the ships to bring the articles from London to New York.

The New York Times, in terms of influence the most important newspaper in the United States today, used to be in the Pace University Building at 41 Park Row (see plaque on outer wall).

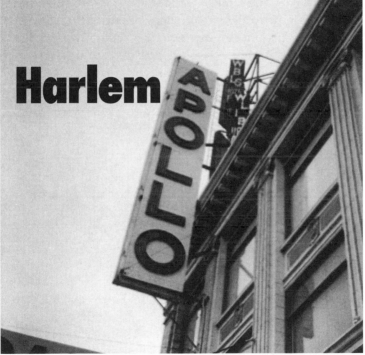

Harlem

PHOTO BY BRUCE KAYTON

Though Harlem includes some of New York City's poorest areas, due to the twin terrors of capitalism and racism, it is one of the most requested areas for tourists to visit in the city, perhaps because it is one of the richest areas historically. By the 1920s, Harlem was known as the "Black Capital of the World." This was during the Harlem Renaissance, when it boasted one of the greatest gatherings of novelists, artists, poets, musicians and playwrights anywhere in the world.

Harlem's population increased tremendously at the turn of the century, as many African Americans fled the racism of the South or immigrated from the Caribbean. The very first subway in New York City came through Harlem in 1904 (following the #3 line above Forty-second Street), bringing the African-American masses to Harlem following real estate speculation and building by the real estate industry.

Harlem boasts A. Philip Randolph, founder of the first major African-American union in the United States, Malcolm X, Marcus Garvey, the Black Panthers, the Schomburg Center for Research in Black Culture, Langston Hughes, Fidel Castro, the Delany sisters (recent subjects of a Broadway play), and the Communist and Socialist Parties. Though there is Jewish, Dutch, Native-American, Italian, and Puerto-Rican history in Harlem, this tour will focus on the African-American history, which is what gave Harlem its current worldwide reputation.

HARLEM TOUR

❶ **306 MALCOLM X BLVD. (formerly Lenox Avenue)**—
This building was the Communist Party headquarters for the Harlem branch in the 1920s and 1930s. Though membership never exceeded one thousand members, over five times that number turned out for rallies. The African-American Communist Party leadership came from the Caribbean and included Cyril Briggs, former founder of the African Blood Brotherhood for African Liberation and Redemption, and Richard Moore of Barbados, who spoke on many Harlem street corners in this era. The Communist Party in Harlem funded trips to the Soviet Union by African Americans and a news service that sent articles to African-American newspapers all over the country.

The Communist Party spoke on street corners and organized rallies without applying for permits. They attracted thousands on issues like the Scottsboro Boys case, where nine African Americans were sentenced to death within two weeks on false charges of raping two white women. This era also saw intense Black-Jewish cooperation; the lawyer representing the Scottsboro Boys, Samuel Liebowitz, was singled out by the prosecutor as a Jew, which perhaps contributed to the loss of the initial case, before it was successfully appealed before the Supreme Court.

African Americans and whites worked together to defend apartments where families were being evicted, and put their bodies on the line over issues important to the Harlem community, such as rent-gouging.

Harlem Tour

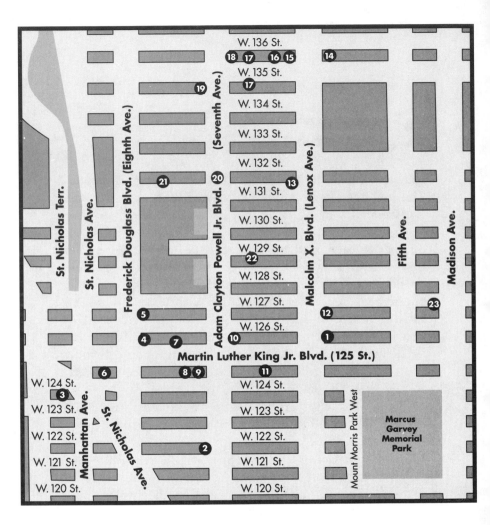

The Communist Party organized Councils of the Unemployed and tenants' organizations. In 1937, novelist Richard Wright, author of *Native Son*, headed the Harlem bureau of the Communist Party newspaper, and wrote in detail about the Communist Party in his less well-known novels.

In 1948, union organizer A. Philip Randolph spoke on what was then Lenox Avenue and 125th Street to urge African Americans to oppose the peacetime draft because of racial discrimination in the Armed Forces. President Truman eventually signed an anti-discrimination executive order, and the campaign was called off. Randolph was expecting to be arrested for making this speech, but was not.

In the 1930s, a young, unknown Communist Party member named Julius Rosenberg worked in a drugstore part time, while attending City University, on then-Lenox Avenue near 125th Street. A middle-aged African-American man was hit by a bus outside, and Julius took him into the drugstore while waiting for an ambulance. Though Harlem Hospital was eleven blocks away, it took an hour for the ambulance to arrive, and the man died right on the floor. As he mopped up the blood, Julius was in shock over how poor city services were in Harlem; he never forgot the incident.

Those wishing to go a little bit out of the way should mark 20 East 125th Street as one of anarchist Emma Goldman's residences in Harlem at the turn of the century, from which she published *Mother Earth*.

❷ THE BLACK PANTHERS FOR SELF-DEFENSE HEADQUARTERS (2026 Adam Clayton Powell, Jr. Blvd, formerly Seventh Avenue; the northern store front)—The Second Black Panther headquarters in New York City opened here in 1969, and featured Dhoruba Bin-Wahad (then Richard Moore), currently out of jail after a long sentence on a trumped-up charge, and Afeni Shakur, more popularly known as the late rap star Tupac Shakur's mother (she was pregnant with him during the famous "Panther 21" trial).

This branch studied Karl Marx, and Lenin's theories of revolution, and emphasized doing practical work in the community; though the Panthers were known erroneously as cop-killers in the mainstream media, they helped children with their homework, established free breakfast programs, and organized tenants.

The Panthers were one of the best hopes for organizing in the African-American community in the United States, but their early success, with twenty-four chapters around the country, led to government repression that included killings, letter-writing campaigns to provoke infighting between east coast and west coast leadership, as well as arrests on trumped-up charges with large bail requirements.

There was a spirited reunion of the Panthers in 1986 at the Harriet Tubman School on 127th Street, a "Panther 21" reunion at the Schomburg Center for Research in Black Culture in 1995, and a group of books have appeared in the last five years by former Black Panther leaders.

A new generation of Black Panthers has been publishing a newspaper and videotaping the police when they make arrests in New York City (monitoring the police in the Oakland, California community was how the Black Panthers started in 1966).

The headquarters building became a community center after this branch was closed in the early 1970s.

Down the block at 2034 Adam Clayton Powell, Jr. Blvd., is The Washington Apartment House, the oldest apartment house in Harlem (completed in 1884).

3   MANNIE L. WILSON TOWERS (corner of 124th Street and St. Nicholas Avenue opposite Hancock Park)—This senior citizens housing facility was Sydenham Hospital (1925-1980), before Mayor Ed Koch shut it down, creating a symbol of the city's neglect of healthcare in Harlem. When it was in the private sector, it wouldn't hire African-American doctors until the 1940s, and was on the verge of bankruptcy when it joined the municipal hospital system in 1949.

In the late 1970s, rather than put money into renovating the building and equipment, the government decided to shut it down due to deterioration. In 1977, mayoral candidate Ed Koch promised to keep it open if he won the election, but like most politicians, he did the opposite of what he said. Herman Badillo, later to become a deputy mayor in the Koch Administration, called Mayor Koch "the most repressive mayor in New York history" for changing his position.

In 1980, upon hearing that a community with inadequate healthcare facilities would be losing one of its major hospitals, thousands jammed public hearings, held on Worth Street. During the 1980 presidential campaign, two thousand rallied at President Carter's re-election headquarters in midtown Manhattan to demand the hospital be kept open.

The Koch Administration decided to close it gradually through attrition, rather than closing it at once, risking community outcry. However, on September 15, 1980, hundreds of people stormed the hospital on its final day of operation, and occupied the administrative wing. Many of the occupiers were members of AFSCME Local 420, led by Jim Butler, who continues to organize demonstrations and fight the privatization of New York City hospitals.

Picket lines formed, and an effigy of Mayor Koch was hung outside. On the second day of the occupation, thirty protesters remained inside, and police put barricades up around the hospital to divide the protesters outside from those inside. The crowd fought through the barricades, and the police started hitting people with their clubs. Thirty people were injured in a ten-minute mini-riot with Mayor Koch showing his sensitivity to Harlem residents by calling them "punks, thugs, and provocateurs."

The next day, over one thousand rallied outside for three hours to support those inside, but after ten days the remaining nine occupiers were peacefully removed by the police. The hospital eventually closed and became the current senior citizen housing facility in 1987. A few days after the occupation ended, Mayor Koch had to cancel an appearance at the

Amsterdam News headquarters. From left to right, Adam Clayton Powel, Jr., Frederick Douglass, and Malcolm X. PHOTO BY BRUCE KAYTON

dedication of the Schomburg Center for Research in Black Culture because of his fear of protests.

❹   *THE AMSTERDAM NEWS* (2340 Frederick Douglass Blvd., formerly Eighth Avenue)—Founded in 1909, this is Harlem's most famous newspaper. Currently a weekly that sticks very closely to the Democratic Party mainstream, and is filled with press releases and photo opportunities for local politicians and celebrities. A six-week strike in 1968 won forty-six workers a twenty-percent wage increase over three years (does anyone remember wage increases like this?).

5 **UNITY FUNERAL CHAPELS, INC. (2352 Frederick Douglass Blvd.)**—The second floor of this building is where Malcolm X's body lay in state for four days after his assassination on February 21, 1965. Twenty-two thousand people filed past to pay tribute to the thirty-nine year-old Malcolm as police were stationed all over the area due to bomb threats made against the funeral home.

Malcolm X was one of the greatest speakers in American history, and his uncompromising political stance led to his brutal murder, in front of his pregnant wife and four children at the Audubon Ballroom on Broadway and 166th Street. His break with Elijah Muhammad and The Nation of Islam cost him his life, but he was also heavily shadowed by U.S. intelligence agencies before he was killed. It is believed he was going to start to work with his long-time rival, Martin Luther King, Jr., the week he got killed; a liaison that was FBI Head J. Edgar Hoover's nightmare.

Malcolm X is buried in Ferncliff Cemetery in Hartsdale, N.Y. Buses leave from Harlem to the cemetery every year on May 19, the anniversary of his birth.

Unity Funeral Chapels, where Malcolm X lay in state after his assassination.
PHOTO BY BRUCE KAYTON

In 1997, the body of Betty Shabazz, Malcolm's wife, also lay in state here after her horrible death.

6 PROPOSED SHOPPING MALL—HARLEM USA! (124th-125th Streets between St. Nicholas Avenue and Frederick Douglass Blvd.)—There have been several proposals for economic development in Harlem; the current one is to build a five-story shopping mall costing $56 million at this site, to include such "great" American corporations as Chase Manhattan Bank, Radio Shack, and Disney.

A convention center for 125th Street, next to the Adam Clayton Powell, Jr. State Office Building, was also proposed in the 1970s. After millions of government dollars were spent on patronage appointments, architects, and lawyers, it was never built.

A different style economic development program was killed in 1994, when Mayor Rudolph Giuliani kicked hundreds of vendors off of 125th Street. Street vendors have been using the streets of New York City as a market since the 1650s, and immigrants have always used peddling as a way to get a foot in the New York City economy. One Hundred-Twenty-fifth Street seems naked and useless without the strong presence of African immigrants selling their wares.

7 THE APOLLO THEATER (253 West 125th Street)—One of Harlem's most famous landmarks (see photo on page 167), the Apollo Theater still features the weekly Amateur Night Contest. Everyone from Bessie Smith, Duke Ellington, Charlie Parker, and Dizzie Gillespie has played the Apollo Theater. Until 1934, it was a whites-only establishment.

In 1971, John Lennon and Yoko Ono played at a benefit concert for the victim's families of the Attica Prison Massacre.

Also, in front of this theater, two hundred members of African Americans Against Violence marched in 1995 to protest the Don King–produced homecoming for boxer Mike

Site of the famous Blumstein's Department Store, a Harlem institution for many years, now closed. PHOTO BY BRUCE KAYTON

Tyson, after he got out of jail where he served time for a rape conviction.

❽ **BLUMSTEIN'S DEPARTMENT STORE (230-238 West 125th Street)**—The old sign of Blumstein's Department Store commemorates the biggest store in Harlem, which moved to this building in 1900. It would not hire African Americans for anything but menial jobs. An eight-week boycott campaign in 1934 changed that policy when Blumstein's hired thirty-five African Americans as saleswomen. (125th Street has been the scene of many "Don't Shop Where You Can't Work" campaigns over the years.)

Blumstein's Department Store was also the site of an assassination attempt on Martin Luther King, Jr. In 1958, during a book-signing, a deranged women knifed him. His life was saved at Harlem Hospital, the stab wounds inches from being fatal.

9 **FORMER HOTEL THERESA (2090 Adam Clayton Powell, Jr. Blvd.)**—This hotel is most famous for hosting a then thirty-four-year-old Fidel Castro in 1960 on his first visit to the United States, a year after overthrowing U.S. puppet General Battista. (In 1971, it was altered to become an office building.)

Castro came to the United States to speak at the United Nations, but ran into trouble. His plane had to take off immediately after landing because the United States threatened to confiscate it, and no hotels wanted to host him and his delegation. When he threatened to camp out on the lawn surrounding the United Nations, the United States Government jumped into action, ordering all hotels in Manhattan to be available to him. He settled on the Shelburne Hotel, but got into a fight with them over how much of a security deposit they required, and on a suggestion from Malcolm X, he agreed to stay in Harlem.

He took forty rooms on the ninth floor, and met with Malcolm X the first night. Soviet Premier Khrushchev met Castro at the hotel, and pro and anti-Castro demonstrators got into fights out front.

A 258-man New York City police guard protected Castro during his stay; only a few short years later, the U.S. Government attempted to assassinate him.

In a public relations move, President Eisenhower invited all Latin American delegations except Cuba to a luncheon. To counter the snub, Castro arranged a luncheon at the Hotel Theresa for all of the hotel staff. He spoke for four-and-one-half hours at the United Nations (one of his shorter speeches).

The building itself went up in 1910. In 1964, at a press conference here, Malcolm X announced the founding of the Organization of Afro-American Unity; it kept offices on the mezzanine level. After Malcolm's assassination in 1965, crowds gathered in front of the hotel before being dispersed by the police.

⑩ ADAM CLAYTON POWELL, JR. STATE OFFICE BUILDING (northeast corner of Adam Clayton Powell, Jr. Avenue and 125th Street)—This government building was erected in 1973, with protesters demanding that local residents be hired to build it. They weren't. Other community members demanded that a high school replace the small businesses knocked down to construct it.

On this street corner, from which Malcolm X spoke many times, was Louis Michaux's National Memorial African Bookstore, whose sign proclaiming there are two billion Black people worldwide served as a backdrop to Malcolm's speeches, and can still be seen in documentaries of and from that era.

⑪ THE STUDIO MUSEUM (144 West 125th Street)—This famous art museum, started in 1968 at a different location on Fifth Avenue, is a welcome relief from the Eurocentric art in most other New York City museums. It sits next to the orange-brick Koch Building, with the word "Koch" still visible on top. Koch's opened in 1890 to serve the German population in Harlem. They too refused to hire African-American workers, or advertise in the African-American press; appropriately, it went out of business in 1930.

⑫ SYLVIA'S (Malcolm X Blvd. and 126th Street)—This world-famous restaurant started in 1962, and offers good soul food and great soulful music at its famous Sunday brunches. Many press conferences held in Harlem, featuring the likes of Reverend Al Sharpton or Reverend Jesse Jackson, take place in a tent set up in front of the restaurant. Others who have eaten here include Winnie Mandela and Muhammad Ali.

13 **LIBERATION BOOKS (421 Malcolm X Blvd., Phone: (212) 281-4615)**—This great bookstore for African-American history and fiction was started on this spot in 1967. The owner, Una, had a bookstore in Guyana.

14 **HARLEM HOSPITAL (corner of Malcolm X Blvd. and 135th Street)**—Healthcare in Harlem starts with the establishment of the Harlem Dispensary in 1868, which served three thousand people annually. In 1907, the original Harlem Hospital opened on Malcolm X Blvd., between 136th and 137th Streets. It was at this hospital that Martin Luther King, Jr.'s life was saved in 1958, after being stabbed at Blumstein's Department Store (see above).

In 1969, the current structure was built, nine years after the money to construct it was first approved. It took so long because of protests over the lily-white construction industry's failure to hire Puerto Ricans and African Americans.

15 **SCHOMBURG CENTER FOR RESEARCH IN BLACK CULTURE (515 Malcolm X Blvd at 135th Street)**—This new structure, built in 1978, houses one of the best African-American history collections in the world. The white building to the west was the original public library branch (built 1905) where all of the greats of the Harlem Renaissance gave readings and did their own reading. Everyone from gay poet Countee Cullen, to the future head of Ghana, Kwame Nkrumah, and Claude McKay spent significant amounts of time here. Langston Hughes walked up its steps on his very first day in Harlem in 1921. Both structures have been combined, so when one is inside it seems like one building.

The library is named for Arturo Schomburg, who was both Black and Puerto Rican; he was active in committees to support Cuban and Puerto Rican independence at the turn of the century. He worked for twenty-three years as a messenger for the Bankers Trust Company, but spent all of his free time collecting writings by Blacks from all over the world.

He established the Negro Society of Historical Research and got articles published in W.E.B. DuBois' *Crisis*. He eventually collected over thirty-three hundred books, and sold them, cheaply, to the New York Public Library system in 1926 for $10,000, more than doubling the library system's Black history holdings. Shomburg became the curator of the collection, and died in 1938; he's buried in Cypress Hills Cemetery in Brooklyn.

The library has excellent collections of A. Philip Randolph's *The Messenger*, Marcus Garvey's *Negro World*, along with a large collection of videos and photographs. There are two exhibition halls, a great gift shop, and a beautiful tribute to Langston Hughes's famous poem *The Negro Speaks of Rivers* in the tiles of the floor outside of the Langston Hughes Auditorium. It has a time line of the lives of Langston Hughes and Arturo Schomburg, which was christened by water from all of the rivers depicted on the floor.

This street corner was the site where Marcus Garvey and A. Philip Randolph spoke from a ubiquitous soapbox. They eventually became bitter enemies—the left wingers and the Garveyites fighting over the right to speak on which street corner.

16 **THE ST. PHILIPS HOUSES (107-145 West 135th Street)**—When St. Philips Church purchased this row of houses in 1911 for $640,000, it was the largest real estate transaction by an African American in New York City history. Previously, the houses had only been rented to whites, but the African-American real estate agents Nail and Parker quickly pulled down a sign announcing the whites-only policy after the purchase.

St. Philips Episcopal Church (214 West 134th Street) was known as the upper-class African-American church, and they joined the increasing number of African-American churches that sold their buildings in midtown Manhattan at a large profit to buy land in Harlem. St. Philips Church, which sold these houses in 1976, was one of the largest landowners in Harlem. The Communist Party protested against the high rents in 1929, and their front group, the Harlem Unity Tenants League, held meetings at the adjoining library.

When he was known as Harlem's premier photographer between 1916 and 1930, James Van Der Zee had his studio in what is now numbered 107 West 135th Street.

Once the Native Americans were cleared out through violence and phony land transactions, the Dutch established Nieuw Haarlem in 1638. The following year, in what today is known as corporate welfare, Captain Jockien Pietersen Kuyter received a land grant of four hundred acres, stretching from 125th Street to 145th Street.

Captain Kuyter signed a peace treaty with the Native Americans in 1645, but eventually had his house burned down and was killed. He had come to New Amsterdam on a boat with Jonas Bronck, who bought five hundred acres of land from the Native Americans, and eventually had the borough of the Bronx named for him.

In 1658, Nieuw Haarlem, named for Haarlem in Holland, was established as a separate village, and by 1790 the census showed 115 slaves, about one-third of the Nieuw Haarlem population, doing all of the essential labor.

17   YMCA (180 West 135th Street, built 1932, and 181 West 135th Street, built 1919)—The older YMCA on the north side of the street is famous for lectures sponsored by A. Philip Randolph's and Chandler Owen's *The Messenger*. In 1921, Langston Hughes stayed here for $7 a week when he first arrived in New York City to go to Columbia University. In 1940, the fifteenth-anniversary convention of founder A. Philip Randolph's Brotherhood of Sleeping Car Porters was held here. In 1928, Black Scholar W.E.B. DuBois organized a theater group in the basement called the Krigwa Players to combat the racist stereotypes of African Americans in the theater world, a legacy still with us.

The newer YMCA across the street is where Malcolm X, then known as Malcolm Little, stayed on his first night as a resident in New York City (1942), as opposed to the trips he used to take to Harlem in between his porter duties on the trains.

⑱ UNIA OFFICE AND BESSIE DELANEY'S DENTAL PRACTICE (2305 and 2303 Adam Clayton Powell, Jr. Blvd.)— Marcus Garvey, the famous Black Nationalist leader, advocated African-American self-reliance through business ownership. He created the Universal Negro Improvement Association (UNIA) which set up small businesses all over Harlem. This building (#2305) housed a UNIA office and printing facility.

In 1919, it was home to the offices of A. Philip Randolph's *The Messenger*. Number 2303 housed Bessie Delany's dental practice, which didn't raise the price for filling a cavity for over thirty years. The Delany sisters became famous in 1993 due to their bestselling book about their previous 100 years of life, including life in Harlem, and childhoods in North Carolina. Some of Bessie Delany's clients included Ed Small and James Weldon Johnson (see below).

⑲ FORMER SMALL'S PARADISE BUILDING (2294 Adam Clayton Powell, Jr. Blvd. at 135th St.)—This building housed the famous nightclub that featured dancing waiters. It was owned by an African American, Ed Small.

Malcolm X worked here as a waiter at the age of seventeen, when he moved to New York City permanently in 1942. He had a reputation in Harlem for being a street hustler by day and the best dancer at nightclubs at night. He was fired because he got arrested giving servicemen the phone number of a prostitute.

He would eventually earn money on his own through various hustles, with the Harlem Narcotics Squad keeping him under close surveillance. After getting into a dispute with a major numbers runner, he was forced to leave New York City for Boston.

Malcolm X's excellent autobiography gives details of his rise from street criminal and ex-con to one of the major American leaders of the twentieth century. As an African-American Harlem resident once said to me: "He talked about white people the way we talked about white people, but only at the dinner table. He did it right in their face!"

㉟   THE TREE OF HOPE MEMORIAL (Center traffic island at 131st Street and Adam Clayton Powell, Jr. Blvd.)— This multi-colored structure in the center of the street commemorates the former Tree of Hope, which was near this intersection earlier in the century.

Tree of Hope. PHOTO BY BRUCE KAYTON

The tree became known as one with magical powers, capable, through a rub of its trunk, of bringing a job as a singer, musician, actor, or actress. Among those who asked for its charm were Paul Robeson, Bill "Mr. Bojangles" Robinson, and Ethel Waters. Of course, so many performers began hanging out underneath the tree that it became a networking center by itself and eventually entire casts of plays were picked here.

In 1934, with over four hundred people in atten-

Marcus Garvey's 1917 residence (second house from left).
PHOTO BY BRUCE KAYTON

dance, the fifty-foot tree was cut down by the Parks Department in order to widen the avenue. The current marker went up in 1972, but the original stump is now on stage in the Apollo Theater, where it is still rubbed by performers for luck.

㉑ MARCUS GARVEY'S HOUSE (235 West 131st Street)—One of the most significant African-American leaders of this century, Marcus Garvey lived in this rowhouse with his wife, Amy, in 1917. He was a major organizer and instilled Black pride in the community, trying to unite Blacks worldwide and creating Black-owned businesses locally. The Black Pride movement of the 1960s owes a debt to Marcus, as do the lyricists of countless reggae songs over the years.

Though he is known for his Back-to-Africa Movement, he really set up businesses in America that kept Blacks here. His famous steamship line was designed to make money, not to return Blacks to Africa. He was born in 1887 in Jamaica, and after a bad experience in support of a printer's strike, he stayed to the right politically most of his life, leading to his condemnation by leaders like A. Philip Randolph and W.E.B. DuBois. He came to America in 1916, spoke on the street corners of Harlem, creating the Universal Negro Improvement Association and publishing *The Negro World*, a newspaper with a circulation that neared, at times, one quarter million.

In 1919, he bought Liberty Hall on West 138th Street; it sat six thousand, and in 1920 played host to the International Convention of the Negro People of the World, which brought together twenty-five thousand people from all over the world over thirty days.

Garvey was a terrible businessman, and his steamship line went bust, costing investors over $750,000 of their hard-earned money. His strong political work, coupled with a lack of business skills, caught up with him as the U.S. Government was looking for any excuse to arrest him—he was eventually jailed for mail fraud connected to the steamship lines. He was pardoned by Conservative Republican President Calvin Coolidge in 1927, but on the condition that he leave the country.

The UNIA, which continues to this day, was in a shambles and Marcus ended up dying poor in England in 1940. However, his legacy, beliefs, slogans, and skills reverberate to this day at countless demonstrations, concerts, and organizing conferences.

㉒   FOUNDING CONVENTION OF THE BROTHER-HOOD OF SLEEPING CAR PORTERS (160 West 129th St.)—This is the hall where A. Philip Randolph held the founding convention of the first major African-American union, the Brotherhood of Sleeping Car Porters, in 1925. Randolph came to Harlem in 1911, and was inspired by the Industrial Workers of the World, a socialist teacher at City College, and Hubert Harrison, a Socialist Party member.

Randolph joined the Socialist Party in 1916, and became a soapbox orator in Harlem on its behalf. In 1917, he started

The Messenger, a socialist publication which published many of the stars of the Harlem Renaissance. In 1920, he got 202,000 votes in an unsuccessful attempt to become the first African American elected to a statewide office in New York.

He left the Socialist Party in 1920 in protest of its neglect of African Americans, later founding, before a gathering of five hundred men, the Brotherhood of Sleeping Car Porters.

The Abyssinian Baptist Church and the *Amsterdam News* supported the union, though many African-American news-papers and churches supported the Pullman Company because of advertising and donation money. The union was not officially recognized until 1937, after a strong push by President Franklin Delano Roosevelt's New Deal legislation.

Randolph continued to be active in the African-American community until his death in 1979. In the 1960s, he threatened to walk out of community meetings if the other clergymen insisted on expelling the young Islamic preacher named Malcolm X. The intersection of 116th Street and St. Nicholas Avenue was designated A. Philip Randolph Square by Mayor Robert Wagner in the 1960s, but currently there is no sign displayed.

The Langston Hughes house on East 127th Street. PHOTO BY BRUCE KAYTON

Take 124th Street east to Fifth Avenue to view the beautiful Marcus Garvey Park on the way to Langston Hughes's house on 127th Street. The park goes back to the 1830s, and contains a cast-iron firetower from 1856, from which firewatchers would scan, when New York City was dominated by wooden structures.

The Black Panthers held classes in the park in the 1960s, and some of the homes surrounding it sell for $400,000-$500,000. The library across the street from the park was erected in 1909, and shows some excellent films on Harlem history and the history of the Civil Rights Movement.

㉓ LANGSTON HUGHES'S HOUSE (20 East 127th Street)—One of the great writers of the Harlem Renaissance, Langston Hughes lived here from 1947 until his death in 1967. His poetry and short stories are read all over the world, and he takes a place in American literature along with his neighbors Countee Cullen, Carl Van Vechten, Alain Locke, Wallace Thurman, Claude McKay, Zora Neal Hurston, and Ralph Ellison. Hughes grew up poor in Kansas and Ohio, but he came to New York City to go to Columbia University, dropping out for financial reasons after his first years. His *The Negro Speaks of Rivers* poem is considered one of the gems of the century, and his first poem to be published in an adult magazine was in W.E.B. DuBois's *The Crisis*, at 70 Fifth Avenue in Greenwich Village.

In the 1930s, he spent a year in the Soviet Union, and was amazed at how little discrimination he faced. He wrote poems attacking the rich, and worked with the local John Reed Clubs, set up by the Communist Party. He visited labor leader Tom Mooney in jail in San Francisco. His *Goodbye Christ* poem said the new Christ is Lenin, Stalin and the peasants of the Soviet Union. He was called before the House Un-American Activities Committee because of the poem, and lost speaking engagements in the South, even though he had become considerably more conservative by the 1950s.

When Hughes died in 1967, he was cremated in Ferncliff Cemetery as a group of mourners held hands and recited *The Negro Speaks of Rivers*. Martin Luther King, Jr. would quote from Hughes, and there are many famous phrases used today that come from his poems, e.g., "A Raisin in the Sun," "Life for Me Ain't Been no Crystal Stair," etc.

A nice ending to an afternoon in Harlem is to eat at Malcolm X's Mosque, in the cafeteria at 116th Street and Malcolm X Blvd., diagonally across the street from the vendor's market, started when the vendors were thrown off of 125th Street.

Central Park

PHOTO BY BRUCE KAYTON

Central Park is a complete gem and it's a miracle the vicious real estate industry has not swallowed it up. Like a TV newscaster's face, it is almost completely artificial. Almost five million cubic yards of soil and rocks were moved in and out to create it, 166 pounds of gunpowder blasted away rugged terrain, and over twenty thousand workers did the initial construction.

Ironically, it costs hundreds of millions of dollars to maintain a natural environment, due to the fifteen million people who trample the park each year, the amount of automobile pollution, and other poisons of modern living.

In the 1890s, automobiles were banned from the park but drove in anyway to contest the law. One hundred years later, bikers held protests in the park, stopping traffic on the main thoroughfares, to demand that automobiles be banned.

The 843-acre park is only the fifth largest park in New York City, and is the safest police district in the city. It contains fifty-eight miles of pedestrian paths, six and one-half miles of roads, and thirty bridges and arches.

CENTRAL PARK TOUR

① **COLUMBUS CIRCLE ENTRANCE (USS Maine Monument Sculpture and Fountain)**—Columbus Circle is considered such an ugly obstacle course that in 1892, when the Christopher Columbus Statue went up, the Italian community demanded another statue of Columbus in the park "where people could see it." The statue was erected on the four-hundredth anniversary of Columbus's landing on Hispaniola. In reality, it celebrates the enslavement and murder of Native Americans that followed the arrival of imperialism's great hero.

Columbus Circle also features the USS Maine Monument, built in 1913 as a tribute to the 260 sailors killed during an explosion on the ship while it docked at Havana Harbor, Cuba in 1898.

The accidental explosion was treated as an act of war by William Randolph Hearst's yellow journalists; the media's treatment contributed to the beginning of the Spanish-American War. As a result, the United States took over Cuba, the Philippines, and Puerto Rico.

Hearst sold enough newspapers to finance the $175,000 cost of the monument, augmenting the large amount of land he owned in the area. His millionaire newspaper rival, Joseph Pultizer, not to be outdone, put up the giant fountain that still exists across from the Fifth Avenue entrance to the park near the Plaza Hotel.

Columbus Circle is where Women's Health Action and Mobilization! (WHAM!) held rallies every October in the

Central Park Tour

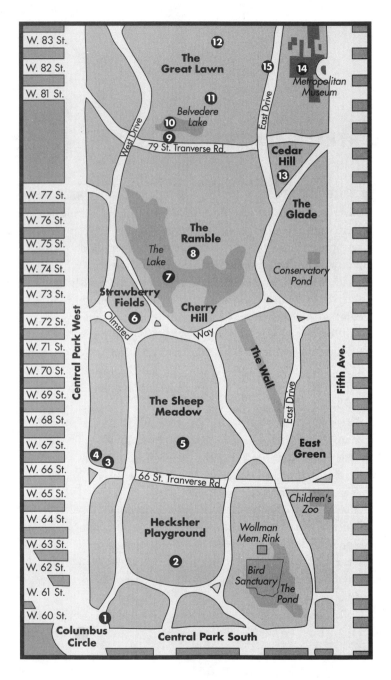

WHAM! counter-demonstration at Columbus Circle, September 29, 1991.
PHOTO BY ELAINE ANGELOPOULOS

early 1990s to counter the Right-to-Life movement's creation of a people-formed cross on Fifth Avenue and Thirty-fourth Street. WHAM! always outnumbered the right-wingers, disregarded police orders not to march down Fifth Avenue, and featured speakers like the Church Ladies for Choice (ACT-UP members in drag), Penny Arcade, and the late Bella Abzug.

Columbus Circle was also the site of a restaurant where the Transport Workers Union was started in 1934 in order to unionize subway, bus, and trolly workers.

② **UMPIRE ROCK (across from the ballfields)**—As one walks through the park, it is important to note the tremendous boondoggle the park was to those who owned land in and around it. As the park was being planned in the mid-nineteenth century, speculators drove up the price of land. Those being taxed for living on the periphery fought tooth and nail to de-value the city assessments of their land. One landowner, Archibald Watt, filed a forty-page complaint against the assessment price of his land, but he made over ten times the original amount back in a subsequent sale.

The city ultimately paid $7.4 million to buy the land that became the park, though pockets around the current reservoir and the Great Lawn were already government owned.

Umpire Rock (see photo on page 191) is so named because it overlooks the field like an umpire. Its Manhattan Schist was formed through millions of years of evolution of the area. One can see ribbons of granite and pegmatite crossing the rock in different patterns. The five-finger pattern on the west side of the rock was caused by glaciers, the last of which came through this area twenty thousand years ago.

Jump across the center of the Umpire Rock and, from the peak, you will see the first children's playground in the park, opened in 1926 with a donation of $100,000 from August Heckscher. There was a debate over whether any rich person should be allowed to designate a structure in the park through a donation.

The rich wouldn't use the playground at first, and there were debates over whether playgrounds or ballfields should be allowed in the park. The rich living around the area thought it would attract the wrong element, the working class, hence destroying their private club. Baseball was also originally banned for this reason, but by 1936, baseball diamonds were put in on the Great Lawn (see below).

❸ TAVERN ON THE GREEN RESTAURANT (A Government Welfare Program for the Rich)—This decadent restaurant is widely agreed to be an unnecessary intrusion in the park. Its monopoly on indoor dining makes it one of the highest grossing restaurants in New York City ($29 million per year in its fiscal year 1993-1994).

The re-opening ceremony, after a $2.5 million renovation in the 1970s, featured a giant ice-cream sundae weighing seven thousand pounds, three bikini-clad women, and the world's largest champagne bottle—about the same height as Abe Beame, then-mayor and perennial Democratic Party hack.

Warner Leroy, the owner, is the grandson of the founder of Warner Brothers Movie Studios. There was a long strike here in the late 1980s, ending in compromise. The joke on the customers here is that they are eating in an 1870 barn for the sheep that grazed the Sheep Meadow across the street; it was a cheap way of cutting the grass.

The sheep crossed the road twice a day, until they were thrown out of the park by Parks Commissioner Robert Moses in 1934, probably because they couldn't be charged a toll to cross the road.

Tavern on the Green was the replacement for the equally gaudy gambling casino in the center of the park. Like its replacement, it had a sweetheart rental deal with the city Robert Moses closed the casino, but loved to have power lunches at the tavern. The tavern is sometimes affectionately referred to as Tavern on the Parking Lot.

❹ TWO CHILDREN'S PLAYGROUNDS (at 67th Street across from Tavern on the Green)—The reason there are two adjoining playgrounds dates back to the Robert Moses era of New York City. From the 1920s to the 1960s, Robert Moses held a dozen different government positions, and was the Czar and dealmaker who oversaw the construction of more than six hundred miles of parkways, bridges, and tunnels, as well as Shea Stadium, Lincoln Center (displacing over four thousand Latino residents), Jones Beach (1931), the 1964 World's Fair, and the New York Coliseum (across from where the tour started). He suburbanized the city and its surrounding area, to the neglect of mass transit. He loved to bulldoze working-class and middle-class neighborhoods, and by the time he died in 1981, his mark was firmly on the New York City metropolitan area.

In 1956, he decided to bulldoze a grassy area adjoining the tavern to add an eighty-car parking lot to Central Park's vista. As was his usual modus operandi, no one was told of the plans, especially the group of housewives who took their children to the grassy plain and nearby playground everyday. When the women of the area found out what was going on by reading the blueprints during the worker's lunchbreak, a full-scale war began.

Moses figured the women would be defeated, as were the 1,350 families living in the path of the Cross-Bronx Expressway in the Bronx whom he had displaced. However, these women lived across the street, on Central Park West, and had money and influential husbands. He tried to bulldoze the area during National Arbor Week at seven in the morning, when he assumed no one would be around, but the housewives were keeping a vigil day and night, and eventually prevented him from building the lot.

To save face, Moses ultimately claimed he was building another playground all along—that's the reason we have two right next to each other.

This was his first major defeat in the public arena, and set the stage for his defeat by Joseph Papp ten years later, also in the park (see below).

⑤   SHEEP MEADOW—This quiet area was a giant dust bowl in the 1970s, before $400,000 was spent to make it into the beautiful grass plain it is today. In 1967, it was the scene of the hippie-sponsored human be-in: ten thousand people being mellow and free. There were no speeches, no leaders, no stage—just people celebrating life in the meadow in brightly colored clothes.

Abbie Hoffman helped organize the event, which followed the 100,000-person-strong human be-in in San Francisco. A giant model of a yellow submarine and giant bananas were passe around. At 6:45 in the morning of the be-in, a police car was pelted with flowers.

1967 also saw a march of several hundred thousand that started here and ended at the United Nations. The Spring Mobilization Against the Vietnam War was led by Martin Luther King, Jr., who had just come out against the war. When marchers approached the United Nations building, local construction workers threw eggs, red paint, and steel rods at them.

Before the march started, seventy people burned their draft cards on the rocks in the southeast corner of the meadow. Over 100 more people joined in, and there were no arrests—an unexpected outcome.

In 1968, the Spring Mobilization attracted 100,000 people with Coretta Scott King speaking in place of her recently assassinated husband. Four weeks before the march, President Johnson announced he would not seek re-election, a victory for the anti-Vietnam War movement.

In 1969, three thousand people participated in a lie-in to symbolize the Vietnamese dead, a tactic popularized by ACT UP in the 1990s in the fight against AIDS and the government. 1975 saw the final anti-Vietnam War protest here when fifty thousand people celebrated the end of the war. Speakers and singers included Dave Dellinger, Elizabeth Holtzman, Richie Havens, Paul Simon, the late Bella Abzug, Harry Belafonte, and Joan Baez. A large banner on the stage stated

A tribute to John Lennon in Strawberry Fields. PHOTO BY PETER JOSEPH

"War is Over," a theme popularized through song by John Lennon and Yoko Ono during their bed-ins.

In 1970, the very first Gay Pride March ended at Sheep Meadow, commemorating the Stonewall riots of 1969 (see Greenwich Village I Tour). It was organized by the Christopher Street Liberation Day Committee, Craig Rodwell, and the Gay Liberation Front. It was hard to get a permit, and the march was very political, unlike those of today. The night before, five gay men had been beaten up in Greenwich Village with the police refusing to press charges. Ten thousand people marched with chants like "Hey, hey, whadaya say? Try it once the other way," and "Out of the closets and into the streets."

6 STRAWBERRY FIELDS—This field opened in 1985 as a memorial to murdered ex-Beatle John Lennon. John Lennon and Yoko Ono took their last walk together here before he was killed in 1980.

Lennon lived across the street at The Dakota (1 West Seventy-second Street) from 1974 until 1980, but his radical period preceded these years, when he did his "Bed-in for Peace" in Amsterdam with Yoko Ono, worked on death-row cases in England, wrote the song *Power to the People*, and worked with several Marxists in England.

He attempted to organize anti-Vietnam War concerts all over the country, culminating with a concert at the Republican National Convention in 1972. His organizing prompted the U.S. Government to attempt to deport him due to an old pot arrest in England, and ultimately, twenty-six pounds of FBI files accumulated on him.

Lennon wrote songs about Angela Davis, took part in the Attica Defense Committee Benefit in Harlem, and hung out in the East Village with Abbie Hoffman, Jerry Rubin, and folksinger David Peel. On December 14, 1980, 100,000 people, as part of a worldwide event, attended a vigil in his remembrance at the Central Park Bandshell.

7 **BOW BRIDGE AND THE LAKE**—This is one of the most famous bridges in Central Park; it was built in 1858, and renovated in 1974. Calvert Vaux, who designed most of the structures in the park, wanted each bridge to be unique, yet fade into the natural landscape. This was the key concept that earned him and Frederick Law Olmstead the winning entry in the competition to design the park.

The lake fills twenty-two and one-half acres and is almost completely man-made. It was famous for ice-skating starting in the 1850s; it was one of the few forms of exercise open to women. The western edge of this finger of the lake was restricted during ice-skating to women only or men accompanied by a woman.

Harassment of women has been consistent throughout human history, and in the 1870s and 1880s, arrests for exposure, sodomy, and rape went up in the park itself.

In 1909, opera singer Enrico Caruso was arrested for 'annoying women' near the Central Park Zoo.

8 **THE RAMBLE**—This thirty-three-acre nature wonderland will have you doubting that you are still in Manhattan. It is a completely planned area, that was designed to have you "ramble" along, passing the one thousand-foot gil (small stream) and perhaps noticing what has become one of the best bird-watching sites in North America.

It has also been a meeting place for gay men since the turn of the century, and in 1947 a young seventeen year-old named Harvey Milk was arrested here during a raid. There have also been violent attacks against gay men, the most famous in July 1978, when a gang sent five men to the hospital, including ice-skating champion Dick Button. Typically, in the 1950s, Robert Moses wanted to pave it over to create a senior citizen's center.

To walk through the Ramble and come upon the Belvedere Castle follow these instructions: Upon exiting the Bow Bridge make the second right, take a left, and walk up the stairs. Then, bear left over a rock in front of a wooden shelter, and make a left turn onto the main path. Follow it along the stream, and go over the concrete bridge (not the wooden bridge) and continue up the stairs. At the intersection, make a right and continue uphill, bearing right at the grassy field. Follow the path counter-clockwise as it circles around the field, passing a giant rock on the right. Go straight on the main path, past the street lights, and up the stairs. On your left will be the instruments that take the Central Park temperature readings, beamed out on the electronic billboard at Columbus Circle, and on the evening news every night. Straight ahead is the castle—hopefully, when you arrive, it won't be rented for a private party; it's a possibility under Guiliani's privatazation policies.

9   BELVEDERE CASTLE (built 1872)—This castle sits on the second highest point in the park, 137.5 feet high. The top tower takes the wind speed and direction readings for the U.S. Weather Bureau. What is a castle doing in Central Park? It was in the original design by Calvert Vaux and follows an English tradition (like the sheep in Sheep Meadow). Looking down into the Turtle Pond gives you a great view of the Manhattan Schist holding you up, which was the southern border of the reservoir that covered the Great Lawn before it was drained in 1930.

10   DELACORTE THEATER (built 1962)—From the castle you also get a great view inside of Joseph Papp's Delacorte Theater, the site of free Shakespeare in the Park since 1962. Joseph Papp's real name was Joseph Papirofsky. He was a former Communist Party organizer from the radical Jewish area of Brooklyn known as Brownsville. He spoke on street corners, sold *The Daily Worker*, and collected money in the subways for the Abraham Lincoln Brigade. Papirofsky moved to Los Angeles in 1946 to manage the left-wing Actor's Laboratory Workshop. It closed after ten years due to attacks from the House Un-American Activities Committee (HUAC).

Papirofsky moved to CBS TV during the Golden Age of Television. The FBI kept their eye on him, but he was able to become a top-notch stage manager and "borrow" crews and equipment from CBS on weekends to put on Shakespeare productions on Avenue D and Sixth Street, and later at the outdoor amphitheater on Grand Street on the East River.

After producing Shakespeare from a flatbed truck in various neighborhoods, Papirofsky started performing in Central Park, which got him into a fight with Robert Moses. Papirofsky used his public relations skills to convince the public that he revitalized the park at night. Robert Moses red-baited him, and took issue with his practice of asking for donations, but Papirofsky won the battle of public opinion, and eventually Shakespeare in the Park became an institution.

However, then-named Joseph Papp was forced out of CBS through harassment after being called to testify in front of HUAC about Communist propaganda in Shakespeare's plays. Luckily, he went on to build the Delacorte Theater, buy the building that became the Public Theater at Astor Place, and put on such productions as *Hair* and *A Chorus Line*, as well as many experimental and political plays.

In May 1982, the Delacorte Theater hosted a nuclear disarmament concert for children in conjunction with the larger June 1982 rally. This concert featured James Taylor, Chaka Kahn and Richie Havens, with the group Performing Artists for Nuclear Disarmament doing skits for the children.

⑪ SENECA VILLAGE (on the Great Lawn approximately between Sixth and Seventh Avenues, from Seventy-ninth to Eighty-sixth Streets)—This former African-American settlement in the park was bought out and/or evicted for the building of the park in the 1850s. African Americans started buying land here in the 1820s, and the AME Zion Church followed, along with its Washington Square Park graveyard.

In the 1830s and 1840s, the construction of the reservoir on the Great Lawn moved the settlement westward, but over

100 families lived here. About one-third of the area was settled by Irish immigrants, ridiculed for living in such a rural
environment. However, the shanties were quite nice, fishing
in the Hudson River was good, and the open space was health-
ier to live in than overcrowded downtown.

In 1850, both squatters and those residing legally were
bought out or forced out, and construction of the park com-
menced. It was extremely intensive, and it took twenty thousand workers over fifteen years to make it into the rolling
meadows and beautiful landscape we know today.

Five workers were killed during the explosions of gunpowder used to blow up the very rocky terrain, and altogether,
over 120 miles of water pipes were laid, six million bricks
used, thirty-five thousand barrels of cement, and 270,000
trees and shrubs were planted.

During the initial construction phase of the park, thousands of largely unemployed workers protested at City Hall
Park, Tompkins Square Park, and in front of the Merchant's
Exchange to get hired. Workers were paid very low wages for
this type of work, and those attempting to unionize were
fired. Only two women helped build the park, and no African
Americans were hired, a condition that has not improved
much in the present-day, lily-white construction industry.

The rich living around the park were constantly attacking
the immigrants, and trying to keep them out. Anything that
went wrong, like crime or garbage accumulation, was blamed
on working-class immigrants.

12   **THE GREAT LAWN**—This space was, before the 1930s,
a reservoir that became superfluous after the $100 million
Catskill System was built to provide water. The field housed
the homeless during the depression, in a settlement called
"Hooverville."

The Great Lawn featured concerts with performers like
Elton John (1980), Simon and Garfunkel (1981) and Diana
Ross (1983), but the most important political event was in

June of 1982 when one million marched from the United Nations to support the United Nations Special Session on Nuclear Disarmament.

Over three million Europeans had marched in Europe in the fall; it fell on United States activists to show the world that the spirit of the 1960s was far from over. Over two thousand volunteers, five thousand New York City cops, and groups like the Vietnam Veterans Against the War, and the Bread and Puppet Theater marched.

No politicians running for office were allowed to speak (a magnificent idea!); those who spoke included Reverend Herbert Daughtry, union leader Victor Gotbaum, Coretta Scott King, and Rubin Zamora, representing the left-wing in El Salvador. Three days after this June rally, sixteen hundred people committed civil disobedience at six of the missions of United Nations countries that had nuclear weapons.

OTHER IMPORTANT SITES IN THE PARK

⑬   CEDAR HILL—This is where the Women's Trade Union League held social picnics in the park as they organized women in the garment industry into unions, and fought against sweatshops like the Triangle Shirtwaist Factory.

⑭   METROPOLITAN MUSEUM OF ART—In the early 1990s, WHAM! blocked the entrances to the men's room to make a statement about the lack of access to healthcare for so many women. In 1970, Mayor Lindsay was confronted on the steps of The Met by the Gay Activist Alliance's Marty Robinson for not speaking out on gay-bar raids and discrimination against the gay community. The Met itself, like many museums in New York City, was built by the rich for the rich; it took over twenty years for the museum to open on Sundays, in 1891, which allowed the working class to use it (though controlled by the rich, it was sitting on public land, and built by public money).

⑮   THE OBELISK—This thirty-five hundred year-old Egyptian treasure was given to the United States in 1879; robber baron William Vanderbilt paid $100,000 to have it moved here. It took nineteen days just to come through the Eighty-sixth Street transverse road in a shaft balanced on cannon-balls.

ABOUT THE AUTHOR

Bruce Kayton has been a political activist for close to 20 years and has been leading tours of New York City for 9 years. He has appeared on National Public Radio, WNYC-Radio, WBAI-Radio, as well as Japanese prime time TV. Kayton's Radical Walking Tours Web site (http://www.he.net/~radtours) receives about 400 inquiries per month. Kayton lives in New York City.